THE FACT OR

GHOSTS

FICTION FILES

FICTION

S0-DPD-991

Anne Canadeo

WALKER AND COMPANY **NEW YORK**

To Amy and Bebe—with gratitude for
their support and encouragement.

Copy 1

CHAPTER ONE:
THE AMITYVILLE NOT-SO-HORRIBLE HORROR

On January 14, 1976, George and Kathy Lutz gathered their three children and fled in terror from their new home at 112 Ocean Avenue in Amityville, New York. The family claimed that they had been terrorized again and again by some evil entity they called "the Horror."

The family had moved into the rambling, Dutch-colonial home only twenty-eight days before on December 18, 1975. What had happened during those four weeks? What nameless, uninvited force had driven the Lutz family from their home?

A short time after the Lutz family fled the house, Jay Anson wrote about their experiences in a book called *The Amityville Horror*. Based on interviews with George, Kathy, and their three children, the book was advertised as a true story of a haunted house. The book was a bestseller and was later made into a movie. But was it true? Did an evil force prey on the Lutz family and perhaps even cause the horrible deaths of the DeFeo family, who had been murdered in the same house in 1974?

A HOUSE WITH AN UNHAPPY HISTORY

About one year before the Lutzes moved into 112 Ocean Avenue, a horrible crime had taken place there. On November 13, 1974, six members of the DeFeo family—a mother, father, two daughters, and two sons—had been shot dead while they slept. Another son, twenty-four-year-old Ronald DeFeo, claimed that an intruder had broken into the house and killed his family. The police did not believe his story, however, and he was accused of the murder. Ronald DeFeo pled insanity, was found guilty, and was sentenced to six consecutive life-terms.

The house stood vacant for a year until George Lutz bought it. But almost immediately, he claimed, strange and chilling events began happening. It began with a foul, overpowering stench and a black slime that stained the bathrooms. Kathy Lutz tried everything, but the slime could not be cleaned off. Later, hundreds of flies swarmed into a second-floor bedroom and the front door was found ripped from the hinges.

There were physical effects on the Lutzes themselves as well. George Lutz claimed that he constantly felt chilled and had to keep a huge fire roaring in the living room fireplace. He began to feel moody, depressed, and angry. He didn't feel like shaving, changing his clothes, or even going to his office. He felt as if something was taking over his personality, he said later, but he didn't know what it was, or how to stop it.

Kathy Lutz broke out in painful, ugly red marks all over her body. George claimed that twice while they were in bed he had woken up to see Kathy floating above the bed. One time, he claimed, she turned into an ugly old woman before his very eyes, then suddenly was transformed back to her normal self.

The family also claimed to have seen glowing red eyes floating just beyond a second-story bedroom window. When Kathy Lutz hurled a chair at the window, they heard the sound of a pig squealing.

The evil force even spread beyond their house. It began to terrorize a priest who they said had blessed the house when they moved in. Jay Anson's book reports that the priest was stricken by a strange illness and the rectory he lived in was plagued by a smothering foul stench that drove all the other priests out into the street.

George Lutz began to feel that an evil entity had caused Ronald DeFeo to kill his own family and that the entity was now trying to possess him as well. Things became unbearable when a large, white, hooded figure visited the family and then later appeared as a horned demon with a disfigured face. Many other events and strange manifestations of the Amityville Horror were endured by the Lutz family.

If, as the book claims, the Lutzes' story is true, the case would certainly have provided psychical investigators with outstanding evidence of a haunting. Experts on paranormal events did investigate the Amityville Horror. But what they discovered was not nearly as horrible, or even as entertaining, as the amazing tale told in the book and movie.

INVESTIGATIONS AND CONTRADICTIONS

Rick Moran and Peter Jordan, investigators of psychic events, went to Amityville, hoping to either verify the story or find out what really happened.

As part of their investigation, they decided to interview people mentioned in the book *Amityville Horror*. They began with the police, who, according to the book, were called to investigate the strange events. One officer, Sergeant Cammorato, supposedly searched the entire house, including a secret room in the basement. However, when Moran and Jordan interviewed Sergeant Cammorato, he denied having ever entered the house while the Lutz family lived there.

How about the priest who contracted the puzzling illness? He is called Father Mancuso in the book, but his real name is Pecorara. When interviewed by Moran and Jordan, he totally denied that he had ever been inside the Lutz home, blessed it, or heard a spirit voice order him to leave the house—all of which is reported in the book to have happened. Checking with the Sacred Heart Rectory also turned up more contradictions to the Lutz story. There had never been any disgusting odor in the rectory, which the book claimed was so awful it had caused the priests to leave the building. The book also told of damage to the front door, garage door, and windows. But none of the local repairmen or locksmiths had any record of being called to the house for repairs, as the book claimed they were.

Other investigators also looked into the Amityville Horror. After visiting the house, Jerry Slovin of the Psychical Research Foundation wrote that his organization did not find the case interesting because the reports were limited to the personal accounts of the Lutzes, which he did not find "at all impressive or even characteristic of these cases."

The Parapsychology Institute of America spent several months conducting research and interviews with those involved in the Amityville Horror. Afterward, Dr. Stephan Kaplan, the organization's director, wrote: ". . . we found no evidence to support any claim of a 'haunted house.' . . . It is our professional opinion that the story of this haunting is mostly fictional."

Other investigators who have looked into the case also point out that certain events, dates, and other details of the story differ between the interviews with the Lutzes in 1977 (before the book was published) and the version that appears in the book.

As soon as investigators took a close look at this haunted house, it was obvious that nothing the least bit horrible had happened in Amityville to the Lutz family. But why had the Lutzes concocted such a bizarre story?

When confronted with these contradictions and the denials of so many people mentioned in the book, George and Kathy Lutz stuck to their story—or avoided interviews. Despite the overwhelming evidence refuting their amazing tale, they have never confessed to staging a hoax in Amityville. In fact, they have claimed that the "Horror" has followed them to other homes, and told of these further hauntings in a book called *The Amityville Horror—Part II*.

Some investigators who have looked closely at the case suspect that George Lutz had several reasons to make up this bizarre story. Lutz had serious financial and family problems. The book mentions that he was worried about paying his bills and was suffering from a great deal of stress. Dr. Stephan Kaplan wrote that although he found no evidence of demons or ghosts, "What we did find is a couple who had purchased a house that they economically could not afford."

It seems that George Lutz removed his family from the house primarily for financial reasons. Afterward, his dark thoughts and the house's grim history may have prompted him to create a tale of haunting and demonic possession—a tale that proved immensely profitable.

Although George and Kathy Lutz denied that the story was false, an attorney named William Weber, who said he had helped create the haunted house hoax, did confess publicly that it was a fraud. Weber, who was the attorney for Ronald DeFeo, had helped the Lutz family gain publicity. He hoped that if people believed the house was haunted, perhaps his client Ronald DeFeo would be granted a new trial on the grounds that some demonic force in the house had caused him to commit murder.

But Weber later sued the Lutzes, claiming that they had not kept a promise that he would help write the book and thereby get a share of the profits. His confession was published by the Associated Press in July 1979. "We created this horror story over many bottles of wine," he said. Weber also said, "We were creating something the public would want to hear about. If the public is gullible enough to believe the story, so be it."

THE GULLIBILITY FACTOR

Nobody likes to think that they are easily fooled. But the fact is that many people believed the "Amityville Horror" story was true. For one thing, it was a sensational story about a subject many people find fascinating and believe *could* be possible. Also, newspapers, magazines, the book, and the movie presented the story as "true life."

Unfortunately, as in the Amityville story and many others, sometimes facts are not properly investigated or verified. Sometimes, even documentation and testimony of expert investigators cannot be accepted as foolproof evidence.

Many people have heard about the "Amityville Horror" and have even read the book or seen the movie. But probably very few have heard about the investigations that disproved it, or know that William Weber confessed that he and George Lutz made up the whole story.

Just because Amityville was proven to be a hoax, it would not be fair or even logical to say that all ghost stories are therefore false. However, it is clear that many extraordinary stories are often believed without questioning the facts.

It is also clear that the media and many people are interested in stories about ghosts and demons, and far fewer care about boring, follow-up reports of mistaken phenomenon, or even a hoax.

THE MOST HAUNTED HOUSE IN ENGLAND? . . . OR A HOAX BY HARRY PRICE?

One of the best-known and most investigated sites of ghostly apparitions was the Borley Rectory, located near Sudbury in Suffolk, England. The large rambling rectory was built by the Reverend Henry Bull in 1863 as a home for his seventeen children. Four families lived there before it was destroyed by a fire in 1939.

Reports of ghosts began the day Reverend Bull and his family set foot in the house. Just about every type of ghostly phenomenon was seen there at one time or another. Apparitions of a nun, a girl in white, and Henry Bull's son Harry were reported, also a coach drawn by two horses. Whispering, cries, scratching, and bell ringing were just a few of the sounds catalogued by the many ghost hunters who visited Borley Rectory.

Many people interested in psychic phenomenon came to investigate the rectory and many books were written about the place. One widely accepted theory for the hauntings was that a monastery had once been built on the same spot where the rectory stood.

The most famous investigator to come to Borley was Harry Price, a psychical researcher who rented the house for a year and conducted experiments there. He wrote two books about Borley, one called *The Most Haunted House in England* (1940) and another called *The End of Borley Rectory,* which were probably the best-known books on the subject.

Price's reports of ghostly activity in the rectory have been questioned, however. Some investigators suspect that Price manufactured a lot—if not all—of his evidence. Why? For prestige and fame as a ghost hunter, perhaps. The question of whether or not Price told the truth in his books about Borley is still being debated.

According to Price, psychic events occurred at Borley Rectory from the time it was first built and occupied by the Bull family. The most frequent and most violent ghostly period, he said, was from 1930 to 1935, when the last owners, the Reverend Lionel Algernon Foyster and his wife Marianne, lived there.

The stories about Borley Rectory, as reported by Price, are widely known and frequently quoted. The rumors and local legends about the Borley Rectory that had been told over the years also helped Price's books to sound valid. It is little known, however, that during an interview in 1958, Marianne Foyster explained that the events at Borley Rectory were no more than a mixture of natural causes, trickery, and Price's own dishonest reporting.

Many of the noises, Marianne explained, were due to the winds that swept through the rectory's drafty, broken-down corridors. Village boys and tramps often entered the vacant parts of the house. The tramps who sought shelter overnight would start small fires in the empty rooms in order to keep warm. Their secretive nightly activity would account for the reports of eerie lights and other sights and sounds. The noises these intruders made, or their unexpected fleeting appearance as they slipped in and out of doorways or sneaked out of the house in the early morning, were often mistaken for ghosts.

The ghost stories and rumors about Borley Rectory were well known throughout the area. But in contradiction to the rumors and reports of Harry Price and other investigators, Marianne Foyster stated quite plainly that she had never seen any ghosts at Borley Rectory, or anywhere else.

The wife of the Reverend G. Eric Smith, who lived in the house before the Foysters, seemed to share Marianne Foyster's opinion. She reported to an investigator named Trevor H. Hall, "I have gone upstairs in the dark at Borley and watched in the supposed haunted room and looked from the windows: the result has always been 'NIL'—only bats and the scratching of rats."

Mrs. Smith told Hall that her family was not terrorized by ghosts at Borley Rectory, but rather by curiosity seekers who trampled her flower beds and broke windows in hopes of catching sight of some of the spirits that Harry Price had made famous after his first visit in 1929.

CHAPTER TWO:
THINGS THAT GO BUMP IN THE NIGHT

Are all ghost reports nothing more than scratching mice or whistling winds? Maybe not, but investigators will agree that a person's state of mind and their own feelings about ghosts will strongly influence the way they perceive and interpret events in their surroundings.

Imagine yourself alone in a rambling old house that you have been told is haunted. What would you make of the many sights and sounds you would hear during the night? The sound of the wind causing a tree branch to scratch a window pane, or a cat hopping off the sofa in the next room might give you goosebumps or make your hair stand on end.

The most common sights and sounds can easily be misinterpreted. Alan Gauld and A. D. Cornell, British parapsychologists, have studied countless ghost reports. They point out that people easily interpret indistinct sounds as meaningful, especially when they resemble the human voice. Countless natural, everyday phenomenon can sometimes sound like whispers, spoken words, singing, moans, or even laughter.

In addition, it may be hard to tell where sounds are coming from, which will cause an imaginative person to picture any number of possibilities. Sounds from a neighboring house or apartment, for example, may echo in a way that makes it seem as if they are coming from a source close by. Or sounds may carry along pipes or other hollow areas in a house. Even certain common animals, Gauld and Cornell point out, can make "the most alarming groans, screeches, snorts, and sounds of heavy breathing."

In regard to raps, creaks, knocks, scratches, and other such sounds, there are also many common culprits that have nothing to do with spirits. Gauld's and Cornell's list of sounds commonly mistaken for ghosts includes a house settling, branches on windows, insects, rats or mice, nesting birds, plaster crumbling and dropping away, plumbing, and heating problems.

Gauld and Cornell also point out that people

often think their house is haunted when they see a door open and close by itself. The sight is truly eerie, especially if one is alone late at night and already believes in ghosts. But the phenomenon is usually caused by a warped door frame or floorboards (quite common in older houses), improperly hung doors, or even a gust of air from the wind or a gust caused by the closing of a door in another part of the house.

Cornell investigated an interesting case in 1966 involving a young couple who had just moved into a new house in Dorset, England. The husband worked nights and the wife was alone with the children. She began to think that there was a ghost in the house who only visited when her husband was at work. A few times a week for several months she heard the front door knocker and the door rattle. Then the door between the living room and hall opened. A few seconds later, the door on the far end of the living room would open into the kitchen. Sometimes she even saw the doorknob turning, she said. Other sights and sounds that occurred around the house late at night also contributed to her feeling that a ghost was visiting.

However, it was soon discovered that the doors opening and closing were caused by a gust of air that was produced when the bedroom doors upstairs were quickly opened or closed. Cornell also learned that the house next door, which had the same design, also had doors that mysteriously opened and closed, especially on a windy day.

In regard to lights or electrical appliances switching on and off, there are many mechanical reasons why this might occur. Sometimes a switch might be weak or partly broken and the slightest pressure will disturb it. Sometimes inside or outside wiring may be loose or worn out, so that the wind or other weather conditions can cause strange things to happen to the lights or even to the doorbells. "These causes may seem trivial and obvious, but it's remarkable what an imaginative person can make of them," comment Gauld and Cornell.

Gauld and Cornell also point out that the personality and intelligence of a witness have a lot to do with a report of a paranormal event. As mentioned earlier, the way a sound or sight is interpreted depends a great deal on a person's expectations or state of mind. A nervous or imaginative person might be frightened by events that another person will not even notice.

Other people simply need the excitement in their life. They want to believe that they are the focus of a paranormal event. Gauld and Cornell note that such people can convince themselves that they are involved in a paranormal happening even when there is absolutely no evidence of special events going on around them.

IS SEEING BELIEVING?

But how about all the people who have claimed to have actually seen a ghost? Isn't that some proof that ghosts really do exist? Professor H. H. Price (not to be confused with Harry Price), who was President of the Society for Psychical Research in England, had this to say about witnesses of ghostly apparitions:

The tea party question "Do you believe in ghosts?" is one of the most ambiguous which can be asked. But if we take it to mean "Do you believe that people sometimes experience apparitions?" the answer is that they certainly do. No one who examines the evidence can come to any other conclusions. Instead of disputing the facts, we must try to explain them. But whatever explanations we offer, we soon find ourselves in deep waters indeed.

APPARITIONS AND HALLUCINATIONS

In other words, Professor Price was not disputing the fact that many people see apparitions. But are they seeing ghosts? Possibly not, if we are defining ghosts as the spirits of deceased persons. But if they are not seeing ghosts, what are they seeing?

Psychical researcher Andrew MacKenzie has one theory. He has written that "nearly all the cases of apparitions collected give every indication that they were subjective and therefore were hallucinations of the senses." A hallucination is an illusion or false perception of objects or events that seems very real. A hallucination is not the same as imagining or day-dreaming. The sights, sounds, smells, or even taste of a hallucination is very real to the person experiencing it.

The Society for Psychical Research in England took a survey about hallucinations and collected answers from 17,000 people. The survey question read: "Have you ever, when believing yourself to be completely awake, had a vivid impression of seeing or being touched by a living being or inanimate object, or hearing a voice; which impression, so far as you could discover, was not due to any external physical cause?" Almost 10% (or 1,700 people) of those who replied said yes, they'd had a sensory hallucination of that kind.

Mr. G. N. M. Tyrell, a psychical researcher, wrote a book called *Apparitions*, which is considered one of the best on the topic. After studying many cases, Tyrell wrote about some common features of apparitions. First, they do not always look like material objects and sometimes appear in a separate space. For example, a wall may seem to fade away and an apparition might appear in the space. The apparitions may also appear and disappear in locked rooms, they may fade away or disappear into walls or closed doors, or they may pass through physical objects. They are often seen and heard by more than one person present, but not all. Tyrell has also observed that it is rare for apparitions to talk. They might speak and even answer a question, but is uncommon for a witness to carry on a long discussion with an apparition.

Why would a person see an apparition? As mentioned earlier, the experience can be the result of a person's state of mind, expectations, desires, and fears, combined with sensory stimulations in their surroundings. For example, it is very common for a husband or wife who has recently lost his or her spouse to imagine hearing or even seeing the lost loved one. The experience may be no more than sensing that person's presence in the house, misinterpreting ordinary noises in the house as footsteps, or hearing the sounds of the deceased person's familiar habits. The senses are tricked by the unconscious hope or wish that the loved one is still alive.

PSYCHIC MOVIES

Haunting apparitions are considered by many parapsychologists to be a type of hallucination. But if they are hallucinations, how can we explain the fact that several different people may report seeing the same or a similar apparition in the same spot?

Some parapsychologists use an interesting

theory to explain the cause of ghostly apparitions. Sir Oliver Lodge was one of several well-respected scientists who studied paranormal events in the nineteenth century. He thought that some apparitions might be a strange kind of recording caused by dramatic events or tragic emotions that happened at a certain spot. He thought that somehow these intense human emotions caused the image of the event or person involved to be imprinted on the surrounding environment. In other words, people may actually be seeing an image of a deceased person. But that image or apparition is not the person's soul or spirit. It is only image, like the images that flicker across the screen during a movie.

Taking this idea a bit further, Colin Wilson has pointed out that in the many thousands of cases of ghostly apparitions on file with the Society for Psychical Research, "the majority of ghosts do not seem to notice the onlookers . . . In fact, they behave exactly as if they are a kind of film projection." In many cases, he points out, the ghost might be seen wandering across a room, looking anxious, or reenacting some past event over and over again. Colin considers the purposeless and repetitive behavior of most apparitions to be more proof that these sights are not spirits or an active entity.

Many people who study paranormal events agree with this theory. How this "psychic movie" is imprinted remains a mystery. Some explanations involve the amount of water or electromagnetic energy at the haunted spot. Some experts also feel that, like photographs, these apparitions tend to fade with time so that ghosts seen during the seventeenth and eighteenth centuries are reported less often these days, or not at all.

Another curious aspect of psychic movies is that some people seem to have a special sensitivity that allows them to see these apparitions, while other people can be in the same room at the same time and see nothing. Parapsychologists believe that this ability may be related to psychic powers, such as telepathy (the ability to read other people's thoughts) or psychometry (the ability to read the history of an object, where it has been, people who have owned it, etc. by touching it). Have any of these psychic powers been conclusively proven? The answer is no. However, that is still not saying that such abilities, certainly beyond the normal range, do not exist.

"SMILE FOR THE CAMERA, PLEASE, AND JUST SAY BOO!"

As we've pointed out above, even if apparitions do exist, it does not automatically follow that these visual events are the spirits of deceased persons. A photograph of such an apparition would provide some evidence to help prove it is indeed the spirit of a dead person. There are few photographs of ghosts, however, which is not surprising when you think of how wispy, insubstantial, and generally unphotogenic they are by nature. Lots of people have come forth with a photograph they claim shows a ghost, but most are unconvincing. A few have been classified as puzzling, but no photograph has yet convinced skeptics that ghosts do indeed exist.

During the height of Spiritualism in the nineteenth century (which was also the early days of photography), certain photographers specialized in taking spirit photographs. For a fee, a person could sit in the photographer's studio and have themselves photographed with the spirit of some beloved deceased family member, or even someone famous. Sometimes the photographer did not specify the spirits that would show up on the finished picture. These photographers were eventually exposed as frauds. They deceived their naive customers by using cardboard silhouettes of figures or had their assistants, dressed in a costume or a swirl of white sheets, sneak into the picture behind the customer's back.

Ghost hunter Harry Price once exposed a fake spirit photographer who used a different technique. Price figured out that the photographer was producing his bogus portraits by the process of double exposure, a technique of putting two photographs, taken at separate times, on one photographic plate. (If a roll of film has ever gotten jammed inside your camera, perhaps this has happened to you by accident.) When the photographer wasn't looking, Price managed to slip the prepared photographic plate out of the camera and slip in a fresh plate, which he knew had not been tampered with. The photographer was quite surprised when he developed the negative and discovered that the "spirits" had not visited the studio after all during Harry Price's portrait.

As photography became more sophisticated and people became more aware of such fraudulent practices, the popularity of spirit photography faded away. Today, photographs and videos can be produced in complete darkness, using low-light and infrared techniques. Since these advances have not made it any easier to photograph ghosts, those who do not believe in ghosts have become even more skeptical of their existence.

There are a few photographs, however, that are still considered "unexplained" by believers and skeptics alike. One is a picture of the Brown Lady of Raynham Hall. Raynham Hall is a grand English manor house located in Norfolk, England. The ghost of the Brown Lady was first reported there on Christmas Day, 1835, by a houseguest named Colonel Luftus. The ghost disappeared almost instantly, but was seen again by him a week later. The Colonel described her as an aristocratic-looking lady wearing a long brown satin gown. Her face shone with an unearthly radiance and there were no eyes in her eye sockets.

Over the next hundred years, the ghost was reported on about three other occasions. In September of 1936, two photographers from a popular English magazine called *Country Life* came to the house to take some photos. One of the photographers had just put a fresh plate in the camera when the other said he saw a ghost on the stairs. The two claim that as the Brown Lady glided down the stairs past them, they took her photograph. After it appeared in the magazine, several photographers examined the negative and said that it didn't seem to be a fake.

However, skeptics consider the story of the photograph's origin and the actual image to be slim evidence that the Brown Lady, or any ghosts for that matter, do exist. Those who believe it is fake point out that the ghost was reported only three times in 100 years, and it seems an incredible coincidence that the photographers happened to be there for one of its rare appearances. Also, the magazine had a lot to gain by publishing a photograph of a legendary English country house ghost.

VOICES FROM BEYOND

Italian scientist Guglielmo Marconi, inventor of the wireless radio, hoped that he could also invent a device that would pick up the voices of spirits. He worked secretly on the invention until his death in 1937.

Thomas A. Edison, inventor of the phonograph and the light bulb, also hoped to devise some electronic means of communicating with the unseen world. He imagined there was a radio frequency between long and short waves that would enable the living to communicate with the dead.

Neither Marconi nor Edison successfully completed these inventions. However, in recent years some people have claimed to have received messages from the spirit world on ordinary tape recorders, as well as through special inventions like those that Marconi and Edison envisioned. During the 1960s, Konstantin Raudive, a psychologist interested in paranormal phenomenon, experimented with recording tape and more complicated electronic equipment. With the help of electronic engineers, Raudive designed a device he called a goniometer, which he believed received voices from the dead. Raudive claimed that the voices he recorded on these tapes spoke in a mixture of several languages at once, and that in order to understand them a listener had to be trained and the voices had to be amplified and analyzed.

But to some skeptical listeners, the "voices" sound merely like electronic static. In 1970 and 1971, an English college student named David

Ellis received a grant from Cambridge University to study reports of recorded spirit voices. A few years later in an article published in *Psychic* magazine, Ellis stated that he thought many of the voices were radio transmissions and not spirits. He wrote, "The air is full of broadcast transmissions—commercial and amateur radio, radio telephony, scrambled speech—no wave length in the normal range can be guaranteed to be clear . . ." However, Ellis also thought that some of the voices on the tape were perhaps transmitted telekinetically from or through Raudive. In other words, Ellis suggested that the spirit voices were not picked up by Raudive's complicated mechanism, but by Raudive himself and then projected in some unexplained way onto the tape recorder. But many people would still be inclined to think that all the voices were radio transmissions.

CHAPTER THREE:
POLTERGEIST—MIND OVER MATTER?

Ghost reports seem to fall into two main categories. The first, which we have already looked at, is a haunting or apparition. These phantom images are usually seen in the same location—a house (often a single room or area of the house) or a certain spot outdoors. We have considered some explanations and theories about this phenomenon.

The second type of ghostly activity is known as a poltergeist. *Poltergeist* is a German word that means "noisy spirit"—an apt description for this type of activity. Poltergeist events are much more common than apparitions. Many hundreds of cases have been reported for over a thousand years.

The main difference between haunting apparitions and poltergeists is that apparitions almost always occur at a specific location, while poltergeist activity seems to occur most often around a specific person, known as a focus or agent. Wherever the poltergeist focus goes, the poltergeist activity almost always follows.

A poltergeist is usually invisible, but its effects can be seen, heard, felt, and sometimes even smelled. Poltergeist activity usually begins with a minor event—some knocking, scratching, or rapping noises in a wall. The activity will usually build to include an entire range of crashing and thumping sounds, flying dishes and furniture, spontaneous fires, unexplainable floods, and puzzling pranks such as rumpled bedclothes or curtains and clothing tied in knots.

Human-like sounds such as moaning, laughter, sobs, screams, or footsteps may be heard. Sometimes an apparition of a ghostly figure will also be part of a disturbance that includes poltergeist activity.

Most poltergeists are not active very long. Often, the disturbances occur for only a few weeks. But sometimes they will last for months, or even for as long as a year.

THE NEWARK POLTERGEIST

May 6, 1961, was Ernest Rivers's thirteenth birthday. He was sitting quietly, doing his homework, when a pepper shaker suddenly came sailing through the air and crashed down next to him. A weird way to be interrupted from homework, you might say. Most teachers would have a hard time believing that a student didn't finish an assignment because something ghostly was going on in their kitchen. But that's exactly what happened to Ernest. And the flying pepper shaker was only the beginning.

Ernest lived with his grandmother, Mrs. Maybelle Clark, in an apartment at 125 Rose Street in Newark, New Jersey. From the night of Ernest's birthday on, cups, dishes, and other objects were flying around the house. Many other witnesses observed the strange events, including neighbors and a psychology professor from New York University. It was no dream, and Ernest and his grandmother could not figure out how to stop it. (For more information about the Newark Poltergeist, turn to page 36 on the other side of this book.)

The events, which became known as the Newark Poltergeist, lasted about two weeks. What was causing all the trouble? Was a mischievous spirit on a spree? Or is there some other explanation for this and other similar poltergeist events?

THE POWER OF MIND OVER MATTER

Most parapsychologists no longer think that poltergeist events are caused by spirits. As strange as it may sound, experts think that a person, not a spirit, is the cause of poltergeist activity. In most cases, the focus of the activity is a girl or boy ranging in age from ten years old to their teens.

In the *Encyclopedia of the Unexplained*, Richard Cavendish offers this explanation for poltergeist activity:

Some persons remain convinced that the . . . phenomenon are due to . . . an incorporeal entity, such as the spirit of a deceased person, or "demon" . . . However, since there is no evidence for such spirits apart from the phenomena themselves, most parapsychologists are of the opinion that poltergeist phenomena are examples of unconscious PK [psychokinesis] exercised by the person around whom they occur.

THE MYSTERIOUS POWER OF PK

Psychokinesis, often called PK, is a term used to describe the power of the mind to affect matter. Since it has been proven that the human body does emit a low frequency of electromagnetic energy, some parapsychologists believe that PK might be a type of electromagnetic force generated by the human brain.

Has this psychic power ever been proven to exist? Some scientists say that it has and some disagree, perhaps adding that PK is certainly possible but has not yet been demonstrated in a conclusive manner.

Dr. J. B. Rhine of Duke University conducted a series of experiments in the mid-1930s to investigate the theory of psychokinesis. Dr. Rhine's subject was a professional gambler who claimed that he could influence the numbers that turned up on dice simply by concentrating on them. The experiments showed that the gambler could, to some extent, cause the dice to turn up sixes.

Since then there have been many similar experiments with people who claim to possess PK abilities. In his book *Poltergeist,* Colin Wilson, a British expert on the paranormal, lists Nina Kulagina, Felicia Parise, Ingo Swann, and Uri Geller as the "star performers" of PK.

Uri Geller is perhaps the most famous person claiming PK abilities. The Russian-born psychic can reportedly bend metal objects, such as keys or forks, with his powers of concentration. Some investigators of parapsychology have doubted Geller's psychic abilities. However, that is not to say that other people do not possess genuine powers of PK.

POLTERGEIST AND PK

The PK of a poltergeist event is much more powerful than demonstrations of PK seen during an experiment. However, parapsychologists believe that the poltergeist focus is totally unaware of his or her power of PK—unlike Uri Geller or other psychics who may possess this ability and practice it at will. In other words, people would not cause these strange events to happen around them—or especially use themselves as the target of flying cups and saucers—if they consciously knew how to control their power.

But some parapsychologists (even those who accept the electromagnetic theories) believe that the powers of PK causing poltergeist events come from a person's subconscious, that deeper part of the mind where dreams, forgotten memories, and many powerful emotions remain hidden from us. Perhaps this is a way of saying that powerful human emotions are a type of energy that can affect matter, just like electricity.

Another explanation is that PK energy for poltergeist events come from the pineal gland, located in the center of the brain. The pineal gland produces hormones that affect sexual development. There is also some evidence that the pineal gland plays some role in higher brain function by secreting the chemical messenger serotonin. When brain cells are deprived of serotonin, thoughts become confused and irrational. Some believe that the pineal gland is also the seat of psychic abilities. A connection between PK or other psychic abilities and the pineal gland has never been proven, however.

When investigators research a poltergeist report, in most cases they find that the poltergeist focus is deeply unhappy, worried, or angry about some problem in his or her life. Unable to express these deep feelings in normal ways, the person expresses these feelings through paranormal channels. Parapsychologists think that the PK expressed during a poltergeist disturbance is a release of these deep, built-up emotions, like a clogged steam pipe that bursts at a seam.

THE HIDDEN EMOTIONS

Let's return to the story of Ernest Rivers. The theory of deep emotions causing an outbreak of PK certainly applies to his case. (Also, look at the poltergeist case involving Virginia Campbell of Sauchie, Scotland, starting on pages 47–51 on the other side of this book.)

Those who investigated the Newark Poltergeist and interviewed Ernest and his grandmother discovered that Ernest had good reason to be deeply unhappy. Neighbors and family members reported that Ernest was likable and well behaved. However, he had suffered some tragic events in his childhood. When Ernest was about six years old, his mother shot and killed his father. She was sentenced to eighteen to twenty-two years in prison. Ernest was sent to live with his grandparents. In 1960, about a year before the poltergeist events began, his grandfather died.

One investigator noted that although Mrs. Clark gave Ernest a lot of attention, she sometimes ignored him or seemed unaware of his needs for affection and attention. For example, on one of Ernest's birthdays, a neighbor baked him a cake, but his grandmother did not even give him a present.

In the case of Virginia Campbell, there was also evidence that the girl had deep feelings of unhappiness that might have been expressed by the poltergeist activity. Virginia was reportedly a lonely child who had only one close playmate and was quite attached to her dog, Toby. When Virginia's father sold his interest in their farm, the family split up and Virginia was separated from the place and faces most familiar to her, including her beloved dog. While living in the house of her older brother, she had to share a room with her brother's daughter, whom she did not like. Since she was in a new school and had little contact with her parents, she would have naturally felt lonely and out of place.

Most parapsychologists will agree that when a poltergeist case is thoroughly investigated there is practically always a deeply unhappy or emotionally disturbed person (usually an adolescent) at the very center of the events.

In some cases, both apparitions and poltergeist events are reported. It is much harder, if not impossible, to guess why and how the two events combine. But if the mind can project psychokinetic energy, there is also the possibility that the unknown powers of the mind can project any number of phenomenon, including sounds, images, or the spontaneous appearance of fire or water.

ANOTHER THEORY EXPLAINING POLTERGEISTS

Of course, whenever a paranormal event is reported, there is always the possibility of fraud. Gauld and Cornell estimate that about eight percent of all poltergeist reports are hoaxes and many more can be explained by misinterpreted natural events.

The "geophysical theory" is another explanation for poltergeist events. Some psychical researchers, such as G. W. Lambert, think that poltergeists are not caused by some unknown force emitted from a person, but from the action of underground water—streams, old sewers, and so on—that run beneath or near the foundation of a house.

Lambert thought that such water might be pushing up at the foundation of the house, particularly after a flood, a hard downpour of rain, or abnormally high tides. The uneven pressure caused by the water at the foundation or underneath the house, he thought, would cause objects to jiggle off shelves, or even fly up in the air if a particularly large, heavy wave hit.

The water might also cause the house to tilt and then, when it subsided, cause the house to drop, which could also cause many poltergeist-like events—not only object movement, but the groans, creaks, and knocking sounds that are often reported.

During his research, Lambert tried to show that poltergeist events clustered around areas near a sea coast or river and near underground rivers (which are known to exist in London). Other investigators point out that there are more reports in such areas simply because there are more people, since large populations tend to settle near a sea coast or river. However, Lambert maintained that even taking the larger populations into account, the poltergeist reports were still more frequent in those places.

CHAPTER FOUR:
MESSAGES FROM BEYOND?

S o far we have looked at several explanations for apparitions and poltergeists and poltergeist events, the two most typical categories of ghostly activity. Some people believe in a third category. They believe that mediums can receive spirit messages from the world beyond.

This is a belief of spiritualists. Modern spiritualists believe that the soul or spirit survives when the body dies, and that the spirits of the dead can communicate with the living through a medium. A medium is someone who is thought to possess psychic powers that enable him or her to see, hear, and feel things others cannot, and to communicate with the spirit world.

But are mediums really in contact with spirits? Many people do not think so. Skeptics of such spirit contact think mediums are purposely or even unintentionally deceptive.

THE FOX SISTERS CONFESS TO FRAUD

The history of modern Spiritualism began in 1848 with mysterious nightly rapping sounds in a farmhouse in Hydesville, New York, occupied by the Fox family. (For the complete story about the Fox family and the beginning of Spiritualism, turn to page 63 on the other side of this book.)

On November 14, 1849, the Fox sisters— Leah, Margaret, and Kate—demonstrated their psychic ability for a small group of people in Rochester, New York, who called themselves spiritualists. After this meeting, the Spiritualism Movement quickly spread throughout America and Europe.

Within six months after the meeting in Rochester, all three Fox sisters were professional mediums and charged admission to their sittings or seances. (For a description of a seance, turn to pages 65–67 on the other side of this book.)

Many people did not believe in the Fox sisters' psychic powers. The young women were investigated by three doctors from the University of Buffalo—Austin Flint, Charles A. Lee, and C. B. Coventry. The doctors and other skeptics thought that the young women may have been producing the rapping and knocking sounds by snapping the knees or other joints. Although the ability to cause sound by snapping a joint is rare, it is not unknown.

The doctors examined the young women and performed some experiments with them to determine if the theory of snapping joints was correct. Although no conclusive evidence of fraud was discovered, from their observations the doctors determined that the Fox sisters were faking the spirit rappings.

In 1851, suspicions of trickery were confirmed when a confession of fraud by Margaret Fox was published by one of her relatives. But Margaret's confession did not seem to have any effect on the growth of Spiritualism. It seemed that people simply wanted to believe that mediums could contact spirits. The movement continued to grow, especially in England.

Some people looked upon seances and sittings with mediums as harmless fun. They paid to see a public as they would pay to see a show, or they held a seance at home for after-dinner entertainment. But others took these beliefs quite seriously, especially if they hoped to contact the spirit of a lost loved one.

In 1861, Kate Fox gave seances for a wealthy New York banker named Charles F. Livermore. Livermore hoped to contact the spirit of his deceased wife Estelle. Kate Fox gave almost four hundred seances for Livermore and was believed to have materialized Estelle's spirit, among other spirits. In addition to whatever form of payment Livermore gave Kate for performing the seances, when the sessions were over in 1871, he also gave her a trip to England.

Many years after her first confession, Margaret Fox confessed again to fraud on May 27, 1888. In a letter to the *New York Herald* she promised to reveal exactly how she, her sisters, and other mediums faked the events in seances. Margaret kept her word and performed on stage at the Brooklyn Academy of Music. She explained how the raps came from her toe joints, and not from the afterworld. Two months later, her sister Kate also confessed and joined Margaret in performances revealing their tricks. Margaret retracted her confession about a year later, but by then most people were unwilling to believe her.

The confessions of the Fox sisters cast a suspicious light on Spiritualism. But the movement was well established by this time, and many people continued to believe that spirit communication was possible and happening all time. Even if the Fox sisters are frauds, Spiritualists argued, that doesn't mean all mediums are frauds.

GAMBOLS WITH GHOSTS: A CATALOG OF SEANCE GADGETS

As Spiritualism became more and more popular, the events that went on during seances became more dramatic. Tambourines and cymbals would sound, tables would rise in the air, phantom hands would materialize, and the medium might even rise from a chair and float around the room above the heads of her guests.

Disbelievers always pointed out that mediums insisted on darkness for these performances, and argued that darkness was a way to hide tricks and equipment. Mediums, however, insisted that darkness was necessary because the strong light was harmful to them once they went into a trance state. Some mediums even preferred to sit behind a curtained area, called a cabinet, that separated them from the other people in the room. They claimed that they needed the isolation in order for their powers to manifest. However, it is not hard to see that the curtain provided the perfect means of trickery.

Fake mediumship was so popular at the turn of the century that a mail-order company in Chicago published a catalog called *Gambols with Ghosts* that listed items mediums could order to fake different effects at seances. One popular item was called the "self-rapping hand," which a medium could make "materialize" at the seance table and "rap" out answers to questions. The hand was usually operated by a string or rubber tubing. Another common way to make a fake hand appear was for the medium to attach the hand to one of her feet, which would remain hidden under the table.

Then, by crossing her legs and pressing the foot up to the edge of the table, an agile medium could make a phantom hand miraculously materialize at just the right moment.

Other equipment for fake mediumship included a stool with a spring-up seat. A medium could agree to be tied to the stool to prove that she couldn't cheat. But once the lights went out, the spring-up seat would rise, placing her in almost a standing position and allowing her greater freedom of movement. She would now be able to reach hidden objects that would allow her to fake events, like the sound of musical instruments.

Another way that mediums gained freedom of movement once the lights went out was to fake touching the people next to them at the seance table.

During a seance, people seated around the table usually hold or at least touch hands by spreading out their fingers on top of the table. The purpose of this is to unite their psychic energies and also to safeguard against any trickery on the part of the medium. However, many untrustworthy mediums knew how to get around this problem. By slowly sliding their two hands closer and closer, they would soon be able to lift their hands away from the table altogether while their two neighbors sat touching each other in the dark, still thinking that they were touching the medium.

Another trickery device was the "spirit rap-ping table." It looked like an ordinary table, but as the catalog described, "When a circle is formed around the table it emits raps as desired. Can be used at any time, no previous prepara-tion necessary. Infallible in every respect." The table was priced at fifty dollars, which was a lot of money in 1901, but a fraudulent medium would also consider that the table would help make money.

SCIENTISTS AND MEDIUMS

By the late 1860s the interest in spiritualism and psychic phenomenon was so widespread that many well-respected scientists decided to investigate. In 1870, Sir William Crookes an-nounced that he would begin to investigate the claims of spiritualists by using scientific meth-ods. Crookes was skeptical about claims of psy-chic powers. Like many others in the scientific community, he thought it was about time that the parlor tricks of seances were revealed.

Another scientist who investigated psychic phenomenon was Dr. Alfred Russell, a natural-ist who had worked with Darwin and contrib-uted to Darwin's theory of evolution. Sir William Barrett, a physicist, founded the Soci-ety for Psychical Research in London in 1882. Sir Oliver Lodge, another well-known physi-cist, also joined in the scientific investigations of the unexplained. Michael Faraday, an eminent physicist, and Thomas Henry Huxley, a biologist, both thought the claims of Spiritualism to be so ludicrous that they would not even consider giving the phenomenon serious scientific consideration.

One of the first mediums to submit to scientific study was Daniel Dunglas Home. Home's psychic feats were reknowned throughout Europe. Home was tested by a committee of scientists in 1869. He changed clothes in front of witnesses to make sure that he had no special devices tucked away in his clothing, and the seance was carried out in a well-lit room.

The only evidence of Home's psychic powers were a few shakes of the table and some rapping noises. Home did not levitate any furniture, materialize spirit hands or spirit bodies, or float around the room above the heads of the scientific committee. Some were disappointed, and some were not surprised at Home's remarkably unspectacular performance. After the medium left, Dr. Edmunds, the committee chairman, showed how easily Home could have shaken the table.

The committee observed Home at three more seances, but the results were the same. In 1870, Home submitted to another experimental test at the University of St. Petersburg in Russia. As a precaution against trickery, Home was seated at a table with a glass top. At this seance as well, Home's psychic powers seemed to have abandoned him.

Skeptics of Home's ability to levitate and float around the room explain that the medium carried out this trick by putting his boots on the ends of his hands and walking slowly with his arms extended straight out from his chest. In a darkened room, he would have appeared to be floating, with his back parallel to the floor. Particularly if the guests at the seances wanted to believe that they were witnessing genuine psychic phenomenon.

Although Home failed to produce spectacular psychic events for scientists, and was even suspected of trickery by some, he was never caught in the act of fraud. In fact, he wrote a book explaining the tricks of fake mediums entitled *Lights and Shadows of Spiritualism,* which was published in 1877.

WILLIAM CROOKES AND KATIE KING

Those who believe in spiritualism and psychic powers sometimes point to William Crookes's research as scientific proof or validation of the subject. However, Crookes's research of two famous mediums, D. D. Home and Florence Cook, has been considered questionable by most experts.

William Crookes, who was one of the first scientists to take a serious interest in psychic phenomenon, was a well-known physicist. Crookes created many important inventions (among them a tube that led to the development of x-rays) and also discovered the element thallium. He began his investigations as a skeptic of psychic powers, but later became convinced that such powers did indeed exist.

Crookes was among the scientists who tested Home in London in 1869. After observing Home and having a private sitting with many of London's most famous psychics, Crookes wrote about his observations for the scientific community. He marveled that Home had caused an accordion to play while holding it with one hand in a cage under the table. But why hadn't Home held the instrument above the table? some asked. Also, wasn't it possible that Home may have secretly held a tiny harmonica in his mouth and that this was the source of the musical sounds?

Many who had thought Crookes was a reliable observer who strictly followed scientific methodology now began to doubt his reliability. Crookes seemed to accept the events without question or proof. The possibility of fraud still seemed so obvious to many who read his accounts.

Crookes's most famous observations were of the medium Florence Cook. During her seances, Florence Cook reportedly materialized a spirit in the form of a young woman dressed in white robes named Katie King. On more than one occasion, Crookes himself walked about the seance room arm in arm with Katie King and even photographed her.

Skeptics pointed out that Katie King and Florence Cook looked remarkably alike. Also, the medium and the spirit were never seen in the room at the same time. Hidden by the curtains or "cabinet," Florence Cook could have easily changed her clothes and then emerged into the dark room as "Katie." Crookes maintained that he had seen the two together, however, and that Florence Cook was so honest and trustworthy that she was actually incapable of such deception.

However, Florence Cook was caught in the act of fraud during a seance in 1880, some time after her sessions with Crookes. She had materialized a spirit girl named "Marie," who appeared in the dark seance room and began to dance around the table. One of the guests reached out in the darkness and grabbed hold of the "spirit's" arm. Instead of dissolving into nothingness, as one might expect a spirit would, Marie struggled to get loose. The gaslights were quickly turned up and there stood Florence Cook, dressed only in her undergarments. People wondered why Florence Cook was not exposed this way when she was studied by Crookes. But perhaps the reason was that Crookes had such unquestioning faith in her powers.

Even after Florence Cook was caught in the

act of deception, Crookes continued to believe in her genuine psychic ability. He believed that most mediums will resort to trickery at one time or another. Such a discovery, he maintained, did not mean that the medium is without genuine psychic powers.

In evaluating the nineteenth-century scientific study of mediums, it has often been pointed out that even the most brilliant scientists of that era were not equipped to detect the means that some mediums used to create false illusions. Also, once a scientist like William Crookes or Sir Oliver Lodge began to believe that psychic phenomenon were possible, they lost their objectivity.

Scientists were apparently often poor detectives when it came to investigating psychics. Many magicians, however, considered themselves to be much better at searching out frauds.

MAGICIANS AND MEDIUMS

Some of the greatest skeptics and most persistent investigators of mediums and other claims of the paranormal have been magicians. The world famous magician Harry Houdini was a very dedicated fraud-hunter. According to one report, Houdini himself had performed as a fake medium for five years before becoming a magician. During his campaign to expose fake mediums, he performed all the so-called genuine psychic feats of mediums through magic tricks as part of his stage act.

Houdini challenged and succeeded in exposing many fraudulent psychics. He said he believed it was his mission to protect the public from fake mediums. However, critics of Houdini said the magician got so much attention from investigating fakers that his real "mission" was free publicity for his stage act. It was also said that Houdini was so determined to prove that all mediums were fakes that he would go to any lengths to discredit them, even so far as to supply the "evidence" of their trickery himself.

Surprisingly, Houdini claimed to believe that spiritual communication might really be possible. He wrote that he had truly sought a valid example of communication from the spirit world, but in thirty years he had not "found one incident that savoured of the genuine."

Houdini was probably the most famous magician to unmask fake mediums, but he was not the only one. Harry Kellar, a famous illusionist, and David P. Abbott, a magician and member of the American Society for Psychical Research, both worked to inform the public about medium trickery. Several books were written on the topic at the time, among them Abbott's book, *Behind the Scenes With the Mediums,* and a book by Dr. Hereward Carrington, *Psychical Phenomenon of Spiritualism,* both published in 1907. These two books reveal

Copy 1

more than one hundred conjuring tricks of mediums. Houdini also wrote several books about his investigations. *A Magician Among the Spirits* is probably his best-known book on the topic.

There are many people today who, like Houdini, are dedicated to investigating claims about paranormal events in order to make the public aware of fraud and misinformation. There is even a society formed for this purpose, called the Committee for the Scientific Investigation of Claims of the Paranormal. Founded in 1976 in Buffalo, New York, CSICOP is an international group of philosophers, psychologists, physical and biological scientists, science writers, and several magicians who think that claims of the paranormal are not being investigated in a scientific way. CSICOP takes the position that no conclusive evidence for the existence of paranormal phenomenon, such as UFOs, ghosts, ESP, and other psychic powers, has ever been supplied by UFO investigators, parapsychologists, and others.

TWENTIETH-CENTURY TRICKERY

In the twentieth century, mediums no longer perform the amazing feats of levitation and spirit materialization that made D. D. Home and Florence Cook famous. In addition to the risks of being exposed by fake-hunters like Houdini, mediums must face technological advances such as infrared photography (low-light photography) that make it much easier to detect fraud in a dimly lit seance room.

Instead, modern mediums claim to use their psychic abilities to establish a mental link between this world and the next. Scientists, magicians, and other investigators continue to study mediums in order to find out if their claims of contacting a spirit world are true.

CHAPTER FIVE:
TELEPATHY, COLD READINGS, AND TWENTIETH-CENTURY DEBUNKERS

Mrs. Leonore Piper was one of the most famous mediums of the twentieth century. Throughout her lifetime she submitted to study by prominent American and English scientists, including the Harvard psychologist Professor William James, Sir Oliver Lodge, and Dr. Richard Hodgson. (For more about Mrs. Piper, see page 71 on the other side of this book.)

Hodgson, who studied and taught law at Cambridge University, had become famous and well respected among other researchers by exposing the trickery of Madame Blavatsky. Blavatsky was a Russian mystic who many believed could perform miracles. Hodgson was sent to India by the Society for Psychical Research to study her. His perceptive observations earned him a reputation as the leading psychical investigator and "debunker" of his day.

When Hodgson arrived in Boston in May of 1887 to study Mrs. Piper, skeptics were sure he would quickly reveal her as a fraud. However, Hodgson became so fascinated by Mrs. Piper's psychic powers that he devoted the rest of his life to studying her.

Hodgson was so amazed by Mrs. Piper's knowledge of his personal life and the lives of other sitters that he hired detectives to see whether they could find out if Mrs. Piper or her husband were secretly gathering information about people. After three weeks of following the couple, the detectives did not discover any foul play on the part of Mrs. Piper. Hodgson was satisfied. He believed that if Mrs. Piper's information was not coming from some outside source, it had to be coming from the spirit world. Since Hodgson had been so successful exposing Madame Blavatsky, his opinion of Mrs. Piper's powers was very well-respected.

SOME DISSATISFIED CUSTOMERS

However, not everyone who visited Mrs. Piper came away amazed at her trance revelations. After visiting Mrs. Piper at the home of William James in 1894, Dr. S. Weir Mitchell wrote to James:

If I had never seen you and heard your statements in regard to Mrs. P., my afternoon sitting with her would have led me to the conclusion that the whole thing was a fraud and a very stupid one . . . On re-reading your notes I find absolutely nothing of value. None of the incidents are correct, and none of the very vague things hinted at true, nor have they any kind or sort of relation to my life, nor is there one name correctly given.

Professor James Mark Baldwin was also invited by James to evaluate Mrs. Piper and remained unconvinced of her powers. He was never even sure she was in a trance. During his sitting he heard "three elements of truth" about his personal life in messages Mrs. Piper had delivered from the spirit world. However, in a letter to James he wrote that this information was "so buried in masses of incoherent matter and positive errors . . . that the sense of her failure on the whole is far stronger with me."

Hodgson and other scientists who believed in Mrs. Piper's powers were not troubled when her messages contained obvious errors. Errors were to be expected if one believed that a medium was connected to the spirit world, somewhat like in a long-distance telephone connection. Static on the line and other interference, they said, made it hard for the medium to always hear the information clearly or correctly. It is interesting to note that Mrs. Piper herself, in public statements, always said that she was not sure whether the dead sent messages through her.

Is there some other explanation for the powers of people like Mrs. Piper? It was clear that she often astounded her sitters with detailed and accurate personal information. If she was not receiving messages from the spirits, as some claimed, what was the source of her information?

TELEPATHY

One explanation for the powers of mediums to supply personal information to their visitors is telepathy, or thought transference. In other words, the medium is not receiving messages from the spirit world, but reading the thoughts of the person who is seated before him or her. Of course, in order to accept this explanation one would first have to believe that telepathy is possible. However, those who do believe that mediums use telepathy to gain information point out that most of the information a medium gives during a sitting is quite trivial and usually known by the visitor.

In other words, a medium might begin by saying something like, "An older woman who was close to you wants to speak." The sitter might automatically think of their mother, grandmother, or aunt—any older woman whom they would expect might want to communicate with them.

If we can accept that the medium has some telepathic powers, then we can probably accept that he or she would be able to pick up some impressions or information from the visitor's thoughts about the specific relative—the color of the person's hair, for example, or their first name or initials.

Investigators believe that the true test that rules out telepathy is when a medium can supply information known only to the deceased person and not to the sitter, and which can later be confirmed as true. (For an interesting story of such a case involving the psychic Eileen Garrett, see page 5 on the other side of this book.)

However, there are very few instances of this type. Even when it does occur, it is still not conclusive proof of communication with spirits. Other psychic powers, like thought transference, could still be at work.

"A BLEND OF FACTS AND FALSEHOODS"?

Again, in considering how amazing or accurate a medium's powers are, one must also consider the sitter's willingness to believe that the medium is truly psychic and in communication with spirits. Vague information that would apply to almost anybody can often be interpreted as personal. It is also important to remember that mediums have several ways of gaining information about a visitor, which they then feed back to the visitor as if it had been acquired through psychic powers.

Let's look at the case of Mrs. Piper. Sir Oliver Lodge, a world-famous physicist who studied psychic phenomenon wrote up a report of his visit with her stating that some of the information she gave amazed him. However, some members of the Society for Psychical Research, who knew the methods used by professional thought readers, did not believe Mrs. Piper had spoken to the spirits of Lodge's deceased relatives.

First, they pointed out that Mrs. Piper usually held hands with her visitors. By holding Lodge's hands, she could feel his unconscious muscular reaction and be able to tell if he thought a statement was true or false. Skeptics of mediums point out that even when a medium does not make physical contact with a visitor, the medium can watch facial expressions or other reactions to tell if their information is on the right track.

The Reverend Thomas Lund, chaplain of the Liverpool School for the Blind, published notes of his visit with Mrs. Piper in the *Proceedings,* a journal published by the Society for Psychical Research. Skeptical of Mrs. Piper's powers, he wrote:

What impressed me was the way in which she seemed to feel for information, rarely telling me anything of importance right off the reel, but carefully fishing, and then following up a lead. It seemed to me that when she got on the right track, the nervous and uncontrollable movements of one's muscles gave her the signal that she was right and might steam ahead.

Lund thought Mrs. Piper's information was "a blend of facts and falsehoods, some meaningful, some absurd." He remained unconvinced that she had been in a trance, used telepathy, or had communicated with spirits.

In the case of Mrs. Piper, those skeptical of her powers agreed that a visitor's first meeting with the medium was the most important. They believed that Mrs. Piper would acquire information through various means during a first visit and then repeat it or use it to gain more information in later sittings.

The methods of gaining information—fishing and watching a visitor's unconscious reactions—observed by Reverend Lund and others who were skeptical of Mrs. Piper are standard "tricks" used by many who claim to have psychic powers. If these tricks are so obvious, why do they work?

A medium's performance can be extremely persuasive, even to someone who considers himself or herself skeptical and objective. But as pointed out before, people who visit psychics are seeking to make contact with departed loved ones or learn more about their future and generally already believe in the medium's powers. They are not watching the medium objectively and are therefore often totally blind to any evidence of trickery. As psychologists have often pointed out, people who are seeking answers to their problems will tend to make sense out of nonsense and may find more meaning in a situation or "spirit message" than is actually there.

Many people believe that mediums are really in the business of *getting* information from clients, although they claim to be *giving* it. Ray Hyman, a psychologist who has taught at Harvard University, has studied the methods of various "psychics"—mediums, tarot card readers, astrologers, and palmists. He defines a "cold reading" as a method used by a "reader" to persuade a complete stranger that the reader knows all about his personality and problems.

First of all, a reader assumes that most people's problems fall under a few general headings: work, health, love, family, money, and so on. Also, the reader assumes that a person has sought a medium (or other type of psychic reader) because he or she needs help with some problem, or simply wants someone to talk to. If the appointment is made in advance, it is possible for the reader to find out information about the visitor. But most readers don't even need to go to the trouble. As Hyman points out, "The cold reader basically relies on a good memory and acute observation."

What does the reader look for? When the visitor first enters, the reader looks at clothing and jewelry (the style and quality). Careful observations can help determine if the visitor is rich, poor, conservative, "artistic," or even shy or an extrovert.

Also, the reader looks at the visitor's physical features—weight, posture, eyes, and hands. The way a visitor speaks or gestures also provides many clues. An accent can reveal that a person was raised in Boston or the Midwest. The use of grammar or vocabulary can reveal a visitor's education or even his profession or interests.

As you can see, a skilled reader can figure out a great deal of information about the visitor in the first few moments of their meeting. Going further, a reader tries to find out as quickly as possible the main problem the visitor is seeking help with. He might do this by "fishing" around in a general way, touching upon the likely areas for problems in everyone's life— love, money, career, family, and so on. By watching the client's reactions—eye movement, body tension, or posture—the reader can tell if he is on the right track.

Also, as Hyman points out, at this point the reader has used trivial information (gained by observation) to make the visitor feel he "knows" all about him and his problems. The visitor begins to trust the reader and lets down his guard. The visitor may even confide in the reader and tell some or even all the details of his problem.

Hyman claims that most readers use the same technique that Mrs. Piper was accused of — feeding back the information "that the client has given him in such a way that the client will be further amazed at how much the reader 'knows' about him." Hyman goes on to observe that, "Invariably, the client leaves the reader without realizing that everything he has been told is simply what he himself has unwittingly revealed to the reader."

There are many other ways that a reader persuades a client of his psychic powers. Readers often deliver even the most ordinary or trivial information they have picked up in a dramatic way. A successful reader will always act confident of his abilities and will act as if he knows much more than he is telling. Once a visitor is persuaded that the reader is obtaining information through paranormal channels, the visitor will also assume that the reader knows everything.

Readers are also good at flattering their clients, which is one of the surest and quickest ways to win a person's confidence and goodwill. Readers are expert at figuring out what a client wants to hear about himself or his future.

Psychologists say that most people are more willing to believe what they *wish* was true about themselves or what will happen in their lives than what is actually true.

When you consider the many successful methods mediums can use to obtain information (and to play upon a client's feelings and expectations), you may begin to suspect anyone who professes to communicate with spirits.

THE BURDEN OF PROOF

Some scientists do not believe that reports of hauntings, poltergeists, or other claims of paranormal events could possibly be true. They think such reports are totally preposterous and should be completely ignored by serious scientists.

Other disbelieving investigators, however, feel that such claims should be disproven. But the danger in deliberately setting out to disprove or debunk something is that a prejudice of disbelief is equally blind to the truth as unquestioning faith.

A third group of scientists and investigators do not believe or disbelieve such reports. They take the position that it is of some value to science to investigate these claims with controlled, scientific methods and an objective, impartial attitude. Paul Kurtz, a professor of philosophy at the State University of New York in Buffalo and founding chairman of CSICOP, thinks scientists should take a neutral position, one that gives parapsychology "a fair and responsible hearing."

As Kurtz points out, some of the most prominent philosophers, scientists, and psychologists of the past one hundred years thought that the psychic realm was worth investigation. Their work, Kurtz thinks, "deserves careful analysis although it is not immune to strong criticism," particularly in regard to the type of evidence upon which these scientists based their claims.

Ghost stories have been with us since man's most primitive era. It is easy to understand why primitive man made up legends and superstitions to explain the mysterious and frightening world. But now that so many mysteries have been explained by scientific and technological advances, some people find it hard to believe that such primitive beliefs—such as in ghosts—persist without any conclusive proof of their existence.

Others will argue that simply because an idea or phenomenon is not proven does not mean it's impossible. However, as Paul Kurtz points out, "The burden of proof always rests upon the claimant to warrant his claim. If all the facts do not support it, then we should suspend judgement."

BIBLIOGRAPHY

Cohen, Daniel. *The World's Most Famous Ghosts.* New York: Dodd, Mead and Company, 1978.

Christopher, Milbourne. *Search for the Soul.* New York: Thomas Y. Crowell, Publishers, 1979.

Frazier, Kendrick, ed. *Science Confronts the Paranormal.* Buffalo: Prometheus Books, 1986.

Gauld, Alan and Cornell, A. D. *Poltergeists.* London: Rutledge & Kegan Paul, 1979.

Green, Andrew. *Ghost Hunting: A Practical Guide.* London: Garnstone Press Limited, 1973.

Smith, Susy. *Haunted Houses for the Millions.* New York: Bell Publishing Company, 1967.

Stemman, Roy. *Spirits and Spirit Worlds.* London: Aldus Books Limited, 1975.

Wilson, Colin. *Poltergeist: A Study in Destructive Haunting.* New York: G. P. Putnam's Sons, 1982.

ASSOCIATIONS CONCERNED WITH PARAPSYCHOLOGY

ENGLAND

College of Psychic Science
16 Queensberry Place, London S. W.7.

Society for Psychical Research
1 Adam & Eve Mews, London W.8.

FRANCE

Institut Métapsychique International
1 Place Wagram
Paris 17.

Group d'Études et de Recherches en
   Parapsychologie
20 Rue Carnot, 92 Courbevoie
France.

GERMANY

Institut für Grenzgebiete der Psychologie und
   Psychohygiene
Eichhalde 12
78 Frieburg, i, Breisgau.

INDIA

Indian Society for Psychical Research
Moradabad

ISRAEL

Israel Parapsychology Society
Ben Jehuda Street 36
Jerusalem

ITALY

Società Italiano di Parapsicologìa
Via dei Montecatini 7
00186 Roma

JAPAN

The Japanese Society for Parapsychology
26–14 Chuo 4, Nakamo
Tokyo 164.

UNITED STATES OF AMERICA

American Society for Psychical Research
5 West 73rd Street
New York, N.Y. 10023

California Parapsychology Foundation Inc.
2580 Adams Avenue
San Diego, CA 92116

Parapsychology Foundation Inc.
29 West 57th Street
New York, N.Y. 10019

INDEX

Abbott, David P., 49–50

American Society for Physical Research, 49, 66

Amityville Horror, the details of, 1–4
  scientists' investigations of, 4–7
  Weber's confession regarding, 7–8

Amityville Horror, The (Anson), 2–6

Amityville Horror—Part II, The, 6

Anson, Jay, 1–2
  Amityville Horror, The, 2–6

Apparitions (Tyrell), 18–19

Apparitions and hallucinations, why people experience, 17–19

Associated Press, 7–8

Baldwin, Professor James Mark, 54

Barrett, Sir William, 43

Behind the Scenes With the Mediums (Abbott), 49–50

Blavatsky, Madame, 52–53

Borley Rectory, 9–12

Brooklyn Academy of Music, 40

Brown Lady of Raynham Hall, 23–24

Bull family, 9, 10
  Harry, 9
  Henry, the Reverend, 9

California Parapsychology Foundation Inc., 66

Cammorato, Sergeant, 4–5

Campbell, Virginia, 33, 34

Carrington, Dr. Hereward, 49–50

Cavendish, Richard, 30

Huxley, Thomas
Henry, 43–44
Hyman, Ray, 59–61

Indian Society for Psy-
chical Research,
65
Institut für Grenzge-
biete der Psychol-
ogie und
Psychohygiene,
65
Institut Métapsychique
International, 65
Israel Parapsychology
Society, 66

James, Professor Wil-
liam, 52–54
Japanese Society for
parapsychology,
The, 66
Jordan, Peter, 4–5

Kaplan, Dr. Stephen, 6
Kellar, Harry, 49
King, Katie, 46–47
Kulagina, Nina, 31
Kurtz, Paul, 62–63

Lambert, G. W., 35–
36

Lee, Charles A., 38–
39
*Lights and Shadows of
Spiritualism*
(Home), 45
Livermore, Charles F.,
39–40
Livermore, Estelle,
spirit of, 39–40
Lodge, Sir Oliver, 43,
48
Piper investigation,
52, 57
rational explanations
for ghosts, 20
Luftus, Colonel, 23–
24
Lund, the Reverend
Thomas, 57–58
Lutz family
Amityville Horror
and, 1–8
George, 1–4, 6–8
Kathy, 1–3, 6, 7

MacKenzie, Andrew,
17–18
*Magician Among the
Spirits, A* (Hou-
dini), 50
Magicians, 48–50

THE FACT OR GHOSTS FICTION FILES

Anne Canadeo

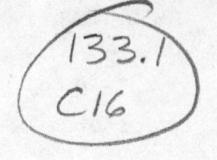

133.1
C16

EAST HIGH
Learning Resource Center

WALKER AND COMPANY ☀ **NEW YORK**

Copyright © 1990 by Anne Canadeo

All rights reserved. No part of this book may be reproduced or
transmitted in any form or by any means, electronic or mechanical,
including photocopying, recording, or by any information
storage and retrieval system, without permission in writing
from the Publisher.

First published in the United States of America in 1990
by Walker Publishing Company, Inc.

Published simultaneously in Canada by Thomas Allen & Son
Canada, Limited, Markham, Ontario

LIBRARY OF CONGRESS CATALOGING-IN-PUBLICATION DATA
Canadeo, Anne
The fact or fiction files : ghosts / Anne Canadeo.
Includes bibliographical references.
ISBN 0-8027-6929-2
1. Ghosts—Juvenile literature.   I. Title.
BF1461.D68   1990
133.1—dc20   90-35871
CIP
AC

Printed in the United States of America

2   4   6   8   10   9   7   5   3   1

Copy 1

To Amy and Bebe—with gratitude for their support and encouragement.

FACT OR FICTION FILES

GHOSTS

CHAPTER ONE:
THE GREEN MAN OF ASH MANOR HOUSE

When Mr. K. moved into Ash Manor House with his family on June 28, 1934, he thought all ghost stories were nonsense. He certainly didn't believe any of the local gossip about his new home. The previous owner of Ash Manor had been so eager to sell the house that he let Mr. K. buy it for far less than it was worth. Mr. K. was suspicious. He thought that something might be wrong with the house, like a leaky roof, but he certainly did not consider that it might have a ghost.

Ash Manor House, a grand, stately house in Sussex, England, was originally built during the thirteenth century. Over the years, some parts of the house have been destroyed and rebuilt.

Surrounded by rolling green countryside, Ash Manor might not look like most people's idea of a haunted house. But the long, interesting history of the house includes scenes of bloodshed, fires, and many other unhappy events. Soon after moving in, the K. family was awakened during the night by strange sounds, as if someone—or something—was stamping its feet and rapping on the walls. Time and again, Mr. K. searched the house in the middle of the night, but found nothing.

THE GREEN MAN APPEARS

Then one night in late November, the sounds came closer to the room where Mr. K. slept. There were three fierce bangs on his bedroom door that left him trembling with fear under his bed covers. Mrs. K., who was asleep in a room nearby, heard them too. The next night the banging came again. Mr. K. lay awake wondering who or what was banging on his door. Two nights later, he found out.

Mr. K. later reported the events of that night to an investigator of ghostly phenomenon: "The room was unnaturally cold and there was something unpleasant about it. I therefore decided to remain awake and see what I could see." Nothing happened and Mr. K. fell asleep. But then, at about three in the morning, a loud bang on the open bedroom door startled him awake.

"I sat up with a jerk," Mr. K. reported. "Standing in the doorway I saw a little oldish man, dressed in a green smock, very muddy breeches and gaiters, a slouch hat on his head, and a handkerchief around his neck. I thought that a servant had left a door open and a tramp had walked in. I challenged him but got no reply. I demanded again what he wanted in my house, and, as he just stood stupidly staring at me, I jumped out of bed and seized him by the shoulder. My hand went right through him. I lost my balance and must have fainted from the shock."

Mr. K. could not remember much after that. He recalled stumbling down the hall to his wife's bedroom, but he was so terrified that he was babbling. Mrs. K. could not understand a word he said, and a few moments later he fainted again. Mrs. K. left the bedroom and ran down the hallway to get some brandy with which to revive her husband. But the Green Man still lingered in the passageway. Mrs. K. related: "His face was very red, the eyes malevolent and horrid, the mouth open and dribbling. He stared at me with the look of an idiot."

However, Mrs. K. did not realize she had encountered a ghost. Like her husband, she thought the horrid-looking little man was a tramp who had somehow wandered into their

house. She asked him who he was and what he wanted. When he didn't answer, she tried to hit him. But her hand went right through him and she smashed her knuckles on the door frame.

Their meeting with the Green Man had been so terrifying that the couple hoped he would never visit again. But that night was only the beginning of the Green Man's visits. In all, they saw him about two dozen times and heard him many other times. The third time Mrs. K. saw the ghost, the old man lifted his head and she could see that his throat had been slashed. The family called in a local priest to bless the house in the hopes that the ceremony would chase the spirit away. But instead of making things better, the priest's visit seemed to make them worse. The Green Man's presence at Ash Manor felt even stronger and more wicked.

Mrs. K. told the investigator: "For two nights I knelt outside my door praying and fighting some intangible force of evil. I have never been so frightened in all my life. It was as if some invisible power tried to hypnotize me. I felt enclosed from every side by evil and almost succumbed."

DR. FODOR INVESTIGATES

The family was so desperate to rid the house of this terrifying force that they called in the help of Dr. Nandor Fodor, a psychoanalyst and leading investigator of psychical events (such as

ghosts, ESP, clairvoyance, etc.). At the time he visited Ash Manor, Dr. Fodor was the Research Officer at the International Institute for Psychical Research in London, one of the few centers for the scientific study of such events. In other words, Dr. Fodor was an expert on ghosts and just the person to call for help in ridding Ash Manor of the Green Man.

As part of his investigation, Dr. Fodor asked the famous American medium Mrs. Eileen Garrett to visit the house. (A psychic medium is someone who many people believe can communicate with the spirit world.) During a trance, Mrs. Garrett learned about Ash Manor from the spirits of the past who lingered there.

During the fifteenth century, she was told, a temporary jail had been built about five hundred yards (the length of five football fields) west of Ash Manor House. The jail was the sight of much human suffering and death. Consequently, many unhappy souls had remained at Ash Manor. Mrs. Garrett explained that if a certain spirit came to trouble someone in the house, it was because of that person's own trouble and unhappiness. The spirit was somehow drawn by that negative, nervous energy and used it to cause even further unhappiness. Many psychics and investigators of paranormal events believe this explanation.

THE GREEN MAN TELLS HIS STORY

During that seance, Mrs. Garrett communicated with the spirits of Ash Manor who had not caused any trouble. But she also spoke with the troublesome, terrifying Green Man, who took possession of her and spoke through her to tell his story.

Dr. Fodor reported that the spirit's voice could not speak through Mrs. Garrett first, however. Mrs. Garrett pointed to her lips, then felt her throat, as if to show that the Green Man was mute because of his slashed throat.

When he finally spoke, it was in words Fodor described as "medieval English." The Green Man pleaded for mercy and caused Mrs. Garrett to throw herself at Fodor's feet. Fodor realized that the spirit had mistaken him for a prison guard. He tried to reassure the Green Man that he would not be harmed and that they meant to help him.

The Green Man identified himself as Charles Edward Henley and told a long, unhappy story. He said he was searching for his son and his wife, who had been taken from him. Henley claimed that Duke Buckingham, a friend from his childhood, had promised him land and money in exchange for his wife. It was not clear if Henley had agreed to this exchange. But he did repeat that Buckingham had betrayed him. Henley was imprisoned, tortured, and mur-

dered. Henley wanted vengeance—he wanted to pay Buckingham back in full for the pain he had inflicted.

Some experts believe that deep sadness or the desire for revenge can hold a spirit to the Earth. Consequently, Fodor and the others at the seance tried to persuade the ghost to give up his hatred for Buckingham. The ghost seemed to relent, then suddenly cried out, "Hold me, hold me. I cannot stay, I am slipping . . ." The spirit's presence faded and Mrs. Garrett woke up.

However, that amazing visit from the spirit of Charles Henley, the Green Man, was not enough to lay his ghost to rest. He soon began appearing again. Dr. Fodor and Mrs. Garrett returned to Ash Manor, and this time they concluded that the spirit was being drawn by powerful feelings of unhappiness in the household.

Mrs. K. finally admitted to Dr. Fodor that she thought this was the true reason for the ghost's visits. She and her husband had many problems in their marriage, as well as problems with their teenager daughter, who had a very violent temper. While the problems existed, the Green Man continued to appear in Ash Manor, and would even take possession of Mr. K. as he slept. However, once the family revealed their problems and faced up to them, the ghost finally lost its power and went away.

The story of the Green Man of Ash Manor

House is considered one of the most fascinating and best-documented ghost stories. Dr. Fodor wrote about the Green Man of Ash Manor House and many other investigations of ghosts in a book called *The Haunted Mind*. Mrs. Maude Foulkes, who had helped Fodor in the investigation, also wrote about the Green Man in a book called *True Ghost Stories*.

But can a ghost story really be "true"? Perhaps after reading this book and learning more about ghosts, you will be able to answer that question.

CHAPTER TWO:
LEGENDS OF THE SPIRIT WORLD

Do you like ghost stories? Those scary tales are usually told just for fun on Halloween or while sitting around a campfire. The tale of a headless horseman who rides up to a mist shrouded castle, or of strange groans and ghoulish laughter heard in an empty, attic room can give you goosebumps. But they are not true, you might say . . . are they?

LEGENDS OF A WORLD BEYOND

Throughout man's history, in every culture and in every part of the world, legends of ghosts have been passed down from generation to generation. Man has always wondered about what happens after death. Almost every culture and

religion has believed that death is not the end. From the Stone Age on, we can find references to the belief that man possesses a spirit or soul that survives death and goes on to some distant, unearthly territory.

During the Stone Age, the Neanderthals buried their tribal members with food and tools, to be used by departed souls in the next world. The Egyptians followed a similar custom. In addition to possessions and tools, however, they placed a small model boat in which the soul could sail safely to the world beyond. The Ancient Greeks believed that souls traveled to another world across the mythical River Styx. Their concept of beautiful Elysian Fields and dark, fiery Hades was equivalent to the Judaic and Christian visions of heaven and hell.

THE NIGHT THAT SPIRITS WALK

Halloween, the holiday we think of when we think of ghosts, has been celebrated for hundreds of years. Halloween was first celebrated by the Celts, people who lived in the British Isles and other parts of Europe. The Celtic religion worshiped nature. Each year on the night of October 31, the Celts celebrated the end of summer and the start of winter with a festival called Samhain.

Samhain also marked the start of the Celtic New Year and honored their god of darkness and death. The Celts believed that on this night,

spirits of the dead rose out of their graves and all kinds of other demons and spooks wandered the earth. The Celtic people hoped to see the ghosts of their loved ones on this night and even left food or other offerings for them.

When the Christian religion later spread throughout Europe, the Church still celebrated Samhain, but renamed it "All Hallow's Eve" or the "Eve of All Saint's Day." (*Hallow* is an Old English word that means "Saint" or "something holy.")

As you can see, many different groups in many lands throughout history have believed in the survival of man's soul after death. It would probably take volumes to tell about all of them.

SPIRITS THAT LINGER

Along with the belief that man's spirit lives on after death comes the belief in ghosts. When people say they believe in ghosts, what they usually mean is that they believe the spirits of those who have departed earth can somehow return and make contact with the living.

One of the earliest ghost stories recorded in history occurred in ancient Greece. The story was told in a letter from the Roman orator, Pliny the Younger, around the first century A.D. According to Pliny, a philosopher named Athendorus rented a house that nobody else wanted. People said it was haunted by a spirit who rattled chains. Athendorus did not believe

the stories and was glad to get the house for such a cheap price. During the first night in his new house, the philosopher was writing at his desk and was deep in thought when he began to hear strange noises. He tried to ignore the sounds, but they came closer. Finally, he looked up and saw a bearded old man with chains on his wrists and ankles standing before him.

Athendorus was frightened, but followed the eerie phantom out to the garden, where it suddenly vanished. Suspecting that some clue to the ghost's origin might be found at that spot, the philosopher had the garden dug up. He found a skeleton with chains on its ankles and feet buried there. The remains were given proper burial and the rattling chains were never heard again.

The old man who haunted the Greek philosopher's house seemed to have had a definite purpose to his noisy nightly visits—he wanted a proper burial. There have been many other reports of ghosts that seem to have a definite purpose to their hauntings, and once it is satisfied they disappear.

STUDYING THE PARANORMAL

Up until recently, ghosts and other odd events were explained by folklore, superstition, and religious beliefs. But in the last hundred years or so, some scientist have become fasci-

nated by the reports. They have chosen to study these strange phenomenon in order to try to understand and explain them.

Ghosts and other strange events that are beyond explanation using known physical or scientific principles are called paranormal events. An event is also considered paranormal when it is outside the range of normal experience or behavior. Predicting the future, telepathy (thought reading), or psychokinesis (using mental powers to affect the physical world) are some, but not all, of the phenomenon classified as paranormal.

Parapsychology is a branch of scientific study that seeks to document, investigate, and explain paranormal events. Parapsychologists believe that simply because paranormal events cannot yet be proven or understood in established scientific terms does not mean that all such reports are merely fantasy.

HAUNTINGS AND APPARITIONS

Parapsychologists find that most reports of ghosts fall into two main categories. The first category is a haunting, sometimes called an apparition. These are phantoms or spirits usually seen in the same location—a house (often a single room, or area of the house) or a certain spot on a road or in a garden.

Sometimes these ghosts are reported to look totally solid and life-like. It is not until much

later that the viewer realizes he has seen, and perhaps even spoken with, a ghost. Other times, such visions are described as wispy and transparent, appearing briefly and then dissolving from view.

Phantasmic figures are usually human, but sometimes they are animals or even objects. It is estimated that twenty percent (or twenty out of one hundred) ghost sightings are nonhuman forms, such as dogs, cats, letters, clothing, and even entire towns.

Although there are many similarities in reports of such visions, ghostly behavior doesn't seem to follow any list of "official" rules. As you will see, there are almost as many different ways that such phantoms appear and behave as there are stories about them.

POLTERGEISTS

A second type of ghostly activity is known as a poltergeist. *Poltergeist* is a German word that means "noisy spirit"—an apt description for this type of ghost. Poltergeists are much more common than apparitions and many hundreds of cases have been reported.

A poltergeist is usually invisible, but its effects can be seen, heard, felt, and sometimes even smelled. Investigators call hauntings and most poltergeist activity "spontaneous cases." In other words, these phantoms and spirits have arrived by surprise, like uninvited houseguests.

A poltergeist will introduce itself with a minor demonstration—a frigid draft perhaps, or some knocking, scratching, or rapping noises in a wall. The activity will usually build to include an entire range of crashing and thumping sounds, flying dishes and furniture, spontaneous fires, unexplainable floods, and mischievous pranks like rumpled bedclothes or curtains tied in knots.

Sometimes the apparition of a ghostly figure will also be part of a poltergeist disturbance. Or there may only be human-like sounds, such as moaning, laughter, sobs, screams, or footsteps. Later in this book we will take a closer look at the long and entertaining list of poltergeist antics. Some are quite unbelievable—even shocking.

LIVING "DOUBLES" AND OUT OF BODY EXPERIENCES

In addition to hauntings and poltergeists, there is also a strange category of rare, ghost-like events known as a "double" case. This is an apparition of a living person seen in one location when the actual person is known to be somewhere else.

There are also many reports of a strange experience by people who have come very close to death and have then been revived. Afterward they have reported the experience of their spirit leaving their body and even traveling to another realm. They described the experience in de-

tail—the sights, sounds, and sensations, as well as who and what they saw in the "next" world. These cases are known as "Near Death Experiences."

Such visions do not fall neatly under the category of "ghosts," but the reports are still interesting to parapsychologists trying to understand hauntings, poltergeists, and the basic question of the spirit's survival.

CHAPTER THREE:
HAUNTING FACES AND
HAUNTED PLACES

Maybe you believe in ghosts. But that doesn't automatically mean you would be able to see one. Ghosts are not visible to everyone. Parapsychologists believe that a person needs to be sensitive in a special way, perhaps even slightly psychic, in order to see ghosts. There have been many cases where a ghost was visible to one person and not visible to another who was at the same location. Of course, there is always the possibility that the ghost was in control and purposely selected his audience.

Ghost sightings seem to fall into various categories. One type of sighting known as a "crisis apparition" has been experienced by people who are far away from the scene of death of a

loved one. It is as if the departing soul wishes to say good-bye to some friend or family member who is unaware of his death. The ghost seen during a crisis apparition usually only appears that one time, and is not considered a true haunting.

A FINAL FAREWELL

Harold Owen, a British painter and writer, had an amazing experience during World War I. Harold was serving in the British Royal Navy and his brother, Wilfred Owen, a famous poet, was an officer in the Army and stationed on the Western Front.

Toward the end of the war, Harold's ship was sailing off the coast of Africa. One afternoon, he went down to his cabin to write some letters and found his brother Wilfred sitting there. Logically, Harold knew that Wilfred was hundreds of miles away, yet there he was. Harold later described the moment this way:

I felt shock running through me with appalling force and with it I could feel the blood draining away from my face . . . I did not sit down but looking at him spoke quietly: "Wilfred, how did you get here?" He did not rise and I saw that he was involuntarily immobile, but his eyes which had never left mine were alive with the familiar look of trying to make me understand; when I spoke his whole face broke into his sweetest and

most endearing smile. I felt no fear . . . only ex-
quisite mental pleasure at thus beholding him.

Barely able to speak or move, Harold
watched his brother for a few more moments.
He again asked Wilfred how it was possible for
him to be there, but Wilfred only smiled. Then,
while Harold glanced away for an instant,
Wilfred disappeared. Exhausted by the experience, Harold slept. When he woke up, he had
an overwhelming feeling that his brother was
dead. It was several weeks later, however, before Harold finally received a letter from his
family sending him the news that Wilfred had
died a few weeks before Harold's strange vision. Harold believed that his beloved brother
had appeared to him one last time to say good-
bye.

Wilfred and Harold Owen were both artistic.
Some believe that creativity such as theirs is related in some way to psychic abilities or the
type of sensitivity required to see ghosts.

SPIRITS WITH A MESSAGE

In addition to ghosts who appear to say
good-bye, there are many reports of ghosts
who have appeared either for some other specific purpose or to send some special message to
this realm.

Take, for instance, the ghost of James Chaffin, who came back to let his family know

he wanted to change his will. This well-documented case is especially interesting because it involved a court decision on the division of the Chaffin family fortune.

James Chaffin of Davie County, North Carolina, died in 1921 and was survived by a wife and several sons. However, his will decreed that only one son, Marshall, would inherit his money and other possessions. As you might imagine, James Chaffin's other children did not think this was fair.

One night in June of 1925, James Chaffin's ghost appeared to his son James and gave him a message. Testifying in court about the vision of his father's ghost, he said:

[my] father appeared at my bedside, dressed as I had often seen him in life, in a familiar black overcoat. He took hold of the coat, pulled it back, and said, "You will find my will in my overcoat pocket." Then he disappeared.

The next day, James searched for the black overcoat, which he found at his brother John's house. In the lining, he found a secret pocket that had been stitched closed. He eagerly ripped it open, but did not find a new will. Instead, he found a note that said "Read the 27th Chapter of Genesis in my Daddie's old Bible."

James Chaffin gathered several witnesses—his daughter and two neighbors—and went to

his mother's house to examine the old Bible. With trembling hands, he turned to the twenty-seventh chapter of Genesis. Tucked between the pages he found a will written in his father's handwriting. This will instructed that the property be divided equally among the four sons and added, "You must all take care of your Mammy."

Despite the fantastic circumstances of the second will's discovery, the court of the State of North Carolina recognized it as legal and decided that it invalidated the first one.

THE GHOST OF NELLY BUTLER

Mrs. Nelly Butler was another famous spirit who returned to deliver a message. Some people think that Nelly's spirit was a bit too nosy and meddlesome because, unlike James Chaffin, Nelly's apparition was seen by many people for a period of over a year in the town of Machiasport, Maine.

One August day in 1799, a strange phantom voice was heard in the home of Abner Blaisdel. The voice identified itself as belonging to the recently deceased wife of Captain George Butler, and gave personal information to prove its identity. The Blaisdels were astounded by this phantom voice, and even more shocked when Nelly appeared to them a few months later, looking much as she did in real life.

By January of 1800, Nelly's spirit began to

appear quite often in the Blaisdel cellar. Probably one hundred or more people saw Nelly's ghost. Many heard her predictions of future events, which later turned out to be true.

Nelly's lively spirit loved an audience, but she said her real purpose in haunting the Blaisdel home was to make sure that her husband married Lydia Blaisdel. The widowed Captain Butler and Lydia were already courting and eventually did marry. Reportedly, Nelly's spirit told Captain Butler to treat Lydia in a loving manner because she would die in childbirth before a year had passed. This prediction also turned out to be true.

The Reverend Abraham Cumming did not believe that anyone in the town had really seen Nelly's ghost. But one day, as if to purposefully shock him into believing in her, Nelly appeared to him alone as he walked across an open field. The vision of Nelly's radiant spirit was totally astounding to Reverend Cumming. He considered it irrefutable evidence that man's soul continues on after death.

Cumming was so moved by his experience of seeing Nelly's ghost that he wrote about the meeting and gathered the reports of many other reliable witnesses who described Nelly's appearances in signed statements. In 1826, he published the record of Nelly Butler's ghost in a pamphlet, which made her the first American ghost whose sightings were recorded in a pub-

lished document. A copy of the pamphlet still exists at Brown University.

EARTHBOUND SPIRITS

Although ghosts such as Nelly Butler and James Chaffin appear for a specific reason, ghosts of this kind are most often not considered true hauntings. That is to say, these spirits appear, conclude their leftover business on earth, and depart, never to be seen or heard from again.

Apparitions that an investigator would consider a true haunting rarely seem to have any purpose. The phantoms or spectres of most hauntings make no effort to communicate with their observers. Most of the time, these spectres are seen repeating some action over and over again in a dream-like or mechanical way. They seem totally unaware that living beings are watching them. If you saw this kind of ghost, you might have the feeling that you were watching a ghostly kind of movie that keeps running over the same frames again and again. Susy Smith, a well-known American investigator of psychic events, thinks that this type of ghost "could be explained as 'earthbound spirits' who wish to continue to live their lives as they did while on earth, perhaps not even realizing that they have died, or if so, not knowing what to do about it."

THE MOST HAUNTED HOUSE IN ENGLAND

The Borley Rectory, near Sudbury in Suffolk, England, was believed to be the scene of many such earthbound spirits and "phantom movies."

The Rectory was built by the Reverend Henry Bull in 1863. Up until it was destroyed by a fire in 1939, it was called the most haunted house in England. The many types of ghostly figures witnessed there included a nun, a headless man, and Henry Bull's son Harry. It is said that Harry Bull claimed to communicate with the spirits of the house while he was alive, and that he promised he would try to return to give some signal of his spirit's survival after his death.

One of the eeriest and most often observed phantoms of Borley Rectory was a ghostly coach and two horses. The coach and galloping horses were often seen and heard racing across the church meadow at night, passing through every obstacle in their way—including trees, shrubs, and stone fences—and then disappearing in the farmyard. Again and again the phantom coach repeated its hurried journey, arriving at one place only to begin again at the start some other night.

These sights and many more were witnessed by the Reverend Bull, his large family, many churchgoers, and other clergymen who lived in

the house in later years. The last owner, Captain W. H. Gregson, reported that on two occasions he went into the courtyard to investigate mysterious footsteps and was followed by one of his spaniel dogs. Both times, the dog stopped in his tracks, then ran away shrieking never to return, apparently driven half-mad from fear.

The apparitions at Borley Rectory were studied by scientists, medical doctors, Royal Air Force pilots, and other investigators. One of the most famous investigators to live at Borley was Harry Price, a psychical researcher who was known for having exposed many reports as fraudulent or mistaken phenomenon. He lived at the Rectory for a year. Price considered the experiments and records he made of ghosts during that time to be quite authentic and "brilliantly successful."

Why was Borley Rectory such a favorite stomping ground for ghosts of all shapes and descriptions? Nobody knows for sure, but some investigators of psychic events think it may have to do with the fact that the Rectory was built on the site of another old rectory. Also, it is thought that a monastery also once occupied the same location. Some psychic researchers feel that the spirits associated with these old structures still haunted the site and took up residence in the new rectory.

STRANGE ENERGY FROM THE EARTH

Some researchers suggest that ghosts and other spectres may be "tape recordings" somehow preserved on energy fields that are caused by water. Sometimes the water may be in a stream that runs beneath the open ground or under a building.

Dr. Margaret Murray, a distinguished archaeologist, Egyptologist, and authority on witchcraft, believed that water and even a humid climate was a necessary condition of haunting. Dr. Murray observed that places with great expanses of sea coast and humid climates, like the British Isles, are renowned for ghosts. But ghosts are reported in arid locations as well, which would seem to contradict the idea.

Another theory suggests that certain spots on the earth are more likely to be haunted or attract ghosts because of the amount of the earth's magnetic energy centered there. Many psychic researchers have pointed out that locations that are continually chosen as sacred sites—the places pagan temples were built or, in more recent times, sites of churches or other places of religious worship—often hold high amounts of earth magnetism.

It is believed that this type of energy passes through the earth in straight lines of force, sometimes called holy lines or ley lines, from the ancient word *lea* meaning "meadow." After

studying these lines of force, many researchers of psychic phenomenon feel that hauntings and poltergeist activity and even sightings of UFOs are likely to occur on them, particularly at a spot where one or more ley lines cross each other.

Psychic researchers are not completely sure what connection ley lines might have to para-normal events. But some suggest that spirits need to draw energy from their surroundings in order to manifest themselves and that ley lines provide an ideal energy source. Perhaps Borely Rectory was so full of hauntings and ghost ac-tivity because it was built on or near ley lines.

AN UNHAPPY END

Another explanation for hauntings suggests that ghosts are the spirits of people who have died unhappily or have experienced a sudden or violent death. Unhappiness or a desire for re-venge, some experts on ghosts say, will cause a spirit to remain on earth. As noted in the story of the Green Man of Ash Manor House, some experts believe that a living person in a bad emotional state will help a ghost to manifest by supplying the energy it needs to appear.

THE PHANTOM ARMY OF EDGEHILL

Houses, churches, prisons, courthouses, schools, restaurants, or theaters—any place can be haunted if it was the scene of intense human

emotion. Ghosts can take the form of a ship, an entire town, or even an army. Consider the case of the phantom army of Edgehill. The country-side just beyond the village of Edgehill in War-wickshire, England, was the location of one of the great battles of the English Civil War. Many soldiers met painful, violent deaths there during the bloody conflict.

For several months after the battle, nearby residents said that they continued to hear the sounds of the fighting armies. King Charles I, who was asked to investigate the matter, as-signed a commission to visit the sight. The commission later testified under oath that mem-bers had witnessed an ongoing phantom battle at the site. Some say the sounds are heard to this day. One researcher who has investigated the site has noted that Edgehill is at the meeting point of ley lines, which he feels accounts for the haunting.

THE HEADLESS QUEEN

The Tower of London, one of England's most famous historic monuments, was built about nine hundred years ago. For many years it was used primarily as a fortress and prison. Conse-quently, it was the scene of thousands of exe-cutions, as well as much suffering, fear, and grief. It is no wonder that so many ghostly ap-paritions have been witnessed there.

The ghost of Anne Boleyn is probably the

Tower's most famous spirit. Anne Boleyn was the second and perhaps best known of the six wives of King Henry VIII. Some said Anne was so ambitious to be queen that she bewitched King Henry. Henry VIII divorced his first wife in order to marry Anne. The divorce was a great scandal and caused tremendous difficulties for Henry. However, he soon tired of Anne and wanted to remarry. In 1536 he had her imprisoned in the Tower, charged with treason, and beheaded.

Anne Boleyn's ghost has been sighted many times in the Tower, with and without her head. Probably the best documented sighting of her ghost occurred one night in 1864. A guard in the Tower saw a woman in white drift out of a room and float toward him. It was the same room Queen Anne had been in the night before her execution. He called out to her to stop and pointed at her with the bayonet on his rifle. The woman did not seem to hear him. She kept coming closer, until finally the frightened guard stabbed at her with his bayonet.

The weapon passed right through her body, as if through thin air, and the guard fainted. He was found later by his captain, who did not believe the story. The captain thought he had fallen asleep on duty and brought him to a military trial.

During the trial two other guards came forward and verified the story, reporting that they

had also seen the ghostly figure approach the first guard. Other witnesses claimed they had seen the ghost near the same room on different occasions. At the end of the trial, the court decided that there was sufficient evidence to clear the guard of charges.

A MESSAGE FOR LINCOLN FROM THE SPIRIT WORLD

Abraham Lincoln, the sixteenth president of the United States, is another famous historic figure who has been sighted as a ghostly apparition. There are many stories of Lincoln's ghost appearing in the White House and walking near his grave in Springfield, Illinois. There are also stories about that the President had important communication with the spirit world before his death.

During Lincoln's time a movement called Spiritualism was quite popular in America and Europe. Followers of the movement believed that the spirits of the dead could communicate with the living through a medium. A medium is someone who is believed to have special powers or psychic abilities that permit him or her to hear spirit voices, and sometimes to see spirits or persuade them to make their presence obvious to others.

Mediums usually communicate with spirits during a seance. A seance is a gathering of several people and the medium, who meet for the specific purpose of talking with spirits. (There

are other ways that mediums exhibit their psychic powers and communicate with spirits that will be considered later.)

Lincoln's wife, Mary Todd, was interested in spiritualism and even held seances in the White House. Mrs. Lincoln became even more interested in the subject after the death of her son, William. It is not known whether Lincoln shared his wife's enthusiasm for spiritualism, but he was known to have attended several seances with her. During one seance Lincoln saw the medium make a piano rise in the air.

Colonel Simon F. Kase, who was part of Washington's inner circle during Lincoln's era, claimed that he was at at least two seances with the President and Mrs. Lincoln. Kase reported that during both these seances Lincoln received a message from the spirit world through a medium instructing him to free the slaves. Kase believed these messages inspired the famous Emancipation Proclamation. The medium, a young girl named Nettie Coburn Maynard, reportedly told Lincoln that a Spiritual Congress was overseeing the nation. According to that Congress, the war would end only when slavery was abolished because spiritual law decrees that all men live freely. Kase wrote about Lincoln's encounter with the medium in a book called *The Emancipation Proclamation. How, and By Whom It Was Given to President Lincoln in 1861.*

THE FATEFUL DREAMS OF ABRAHAM LINCOLN

Lincoln was the first American president to be assassinated. He was shot in a theater by John Wilkes Booth on the night of April 14,1865, and died the next day. Lincoln had served as president throughout the Civil War and died just five days after the war was brought to a close with the surrender of the South.

Some people believe that Abraham Lincoln was psychic and had foreseen his own death in several dreams. Reportedly, Lincoln once told others that in a dream he had seen himself inside a coffin and when he asked what had happened, he was told that the president had been killed by an assassin. The night before he was shot, Lincoln dreamed that he was aboard a ship sailing to a distant, unknown place.

After Lincoln's death, his bodyguard, W. H. Crooks, said that the President had had warning dreams for three nights before the assassination. Why did Lincoln insist on going to the theater that night? No one will ever know for sure. Perhaps he did not believe that the future can be foretold by dreams, or that a person can escape his destiny.

LINCOLN'S GHOST

Lincoln's ghost was first reported by Grace Coolidge, the wife of Calvin Coolidge, the thirtieth president. Mrs. Coolidge observed Lin-

coln's tall, gaunt figure staring out a window of the Oval Office in a pose typical of the deep-thinking statesman.

Lincoln's apparition was also seen many times during the presidency of Franklin Delano Roosevelt. Queen Wilhemina of the Netherlands was visiting the White House during Roosevelt's administration and was quite surprised one night when she answered a knock on her bedroom door and saw Lincoln's phantom standing in the doorway, complete with his stovepipe hat. Much to the queen's surprise, when she told Roosevelt and others about it the next morning, they did not seem at all surprised. They simply explained that she had slept in the Lincoln Bedroom.

About the time of Harry Truman's presidency, Lincoln's ghost was no longer reported wandering the halls of the White House—possibly because the White House had undergone major renovations. Some experts on ghosts believe that ghosts do not like changes in the places they are haunting, or perhaps the changes make it impossible for them to appear.

The spirit of Dolly Madison (the wife of James Madison, the fourth president) certainly did not approve of changes in the White House garden and made her feelings known. The wife of Woodrow Wilson, the twentieth president, wanted to have a rose garden dug up that Dolly Madison had planted. It is said that Dolly Mad-

ison's ghost appeared in the nick of time and scared away the gardeners.

SEARCHING FOR A GHOSTLY HISTORY

Many reports about hauntings and apparitions have been collected and documented. As you can see, some of them even involve the ghosts of famous people. Many others, however, such as Nelly Butler, are the ghosts of ordinary people. Some ghosts, such as Nelly Butler and James Chaffin, appear to people who knew them while they were alive. But that is not always the case. Ghosts of persons who have died a long time ago, sometimes even centuries past, may appear to haunt a house or other location.

These latter cases are very fascinating to parapsychologists. If the ghost can communicate his or her identity in some way, the investigator has an opportunity to check into the history of the house or the surrounding area and verify the information. If records can be found that correspond with what the ghost says, investigators have further evidence to support the theory that ghosts really do exist.

CHAPTER FOUR:
POLTERGEISTS: SPIRITS WITH BAD MANNERS

May 6, 1961, was Ernest Rivers's thirteenth birthday. On that night he was sitting quietly doing homework, when suddenly a pepper shaker sailed through the air and came crashing down right next to him. Ernest was frightened. As he picked up the pepper shaker and stared around the empty kitchen, he felt an icy knot of fear coil up in the pit of his stomach. He knew he hadn't imagined that the pepper shaker had flown across the room. But how in the world could such a thing have happened?

Almost any teacher would have a hard time believing that a student didn't finish an assignment because something ghostly was going on in his kitchen. But that's exactly what had hap-

pened to Ernest. And the flying pepper shaker was only the beginning.

Ernest lived with his grandmother, Mrs. Maybelle Clark, in a four-room apartment at 125 Rose Street in Newark, New Jersey. From the night of Ernest's birthday, cups, dishes, and other objects were often seen flying around the house. Ernest and his grandmother thought they were going crazy. Many other witnesses saw the flying objects, including neighbors and a psychology professor from New York University. It was no dream, but Ernest and his grandmother could not figure out how to stop it.

One night as Ernest and his grandmother ate dinner, several cups sprang out of the punch bowl in the living room and smashed on the floor. At other times, a light bulb unscrewed itself from a lamp in the boy's room and broke on the floor, a bottle of disinfectant flew off a bathroom shelf, and a glass floated out of the kitchen sink and into the living room, where it finally fell and broke as well. The list went on to an exasperating length. Mrs. Clark felt as if she was continually wiping up spills and broken glass. On Friday, May 12, Mrs. Clark and a neighbor witnessed the strangest sight of all—a five-pound iron flew off a shelf in the hallway and swooped into Mrs. Clark's bedroom.

A reporter from the *Newark Star-Ledger* came to the apartment and spoke to several witnesses. He was convinced that the witnesses

were telling the truth and that neither Ernest nor Mrs. Clark was playing a prank for publicity or attention. Also, it was clear that many of the objects seemed to fly toward Ernest, not away from him, which would discount the possibility that he was throwing the cups and bottles when nobody was watching. In addition, many objects took flight far away from the boy and his grandmother, across the room or even in another room.

What was causing all the trouble? The case became known as the "Newark poltergeist." For two dreadful weeks Ernest and his grandmother were forced to share their home with a poltergeist or "noisy spirit." As in most poltergeist cases, the weird, destructive activity faded away as inexplicably as it had arrived. Ernest and his grandmother did not understand it, and they were certainly happy to see it go. As you will see later, the "Newark poltergeist" was rather mild compared to some other cases.

NOISY BUT INVISIBLE

Poltergeists have been reported for over a thousand years. Many hundreds of cases have been recorded from all around the world. Poltergeist events are different from hauntings in many ways. Hauntings most often seem fixed to a certain geographical location. Poltergeists usually focus on a single person, not just a place. The living person at the center of the ac-

tivity is sometimes referred to as a poltergeist agent.

One of the most obvious differences between hauntings and poltergeists is that during poltergeist activity a phantom or spectre is rarely seen. A poltergeist disturbance is heard, felt, and sometimes even smelled, but only the effects of its presence—like the flying cups and dishes in Newark—can be observed.

Poltergeist activity usually takes the form of noise or object movement. Noises range from percussive-sounding raps in a wall, to loud thumps, crashes, and bangs, and even the sound of heavy footsteps. Sometimes a musical instrument will be heard, or the sound of a human voice—crying, screaming, whispering, or even laughing.

Small to very large objects will float, fly, tip, or shimmy off a shelf or table, or fly out of locked cupboards or closets. In some cases, objects such as small stones have been known to materialize and actually rain down on a specific site.

PENNIES AND POTATOES

Small stones falling from the sky would be a strange sight. They are a typical manifestation of poltergeist activity, however, and are often reported. The stones seem to materialize out of thin air and sometimes even rain down *inside* a house. It is hard to imagine such a sight. But

could you imagine pennies or even potatoes hurtling down from the clear blue sky?

The family of Mr. Henry Robinson, who lived in Battersea, a suburb of London, was quite puzzled when pennies showered on their house from November 1927 to January 1928. This was not a very long time, only three months altogether. But it was long enough to leave their home looking as if something—a small tornado perhaps—had deliberately gone on a smashing spree, breaking windows, smashing furniture, and leaving bits of broken crockery in its wake.

The disturbance began outside. At first lumps of coal and pennies rained down on a small lean-to building at the rear of the house. The objects fell at various times for about a month. The family called the police, and the officer who came to investigate could not believe his eyes when he saw bits of coal and pennies ricochet off the conservatory roof. One piece of coal even hit the officer on the head. The area was checked for pranksters, who might possibly be throwing the objects over the garden wall or from the houses nearby, but no mischief makers were found. There was nothing the policeman could do to help, and the Robinsons were left to put up with this strange phenomenon as best they could.

When red-hot cinders were found in the outhouse, the police were called again. This time,

an officer stood watching the yard with a few family members as two potatoes flew into the kitchen, materializing as if out of thin air.

The disturbances in the Robinsons' home soon became worse. Loud banging sounds were heard throughout the house, windows were smashed, and heavy pieces of furniture crashed over on the floor. One Sunday afternoon as the family tried to prepare for dinner, they were terrified as a row of chairs marched down the hall under their own power and piled themselves on top of the table.

As noted in other cases, the bizarre manifestations gradually faded out. However, by that time many of the family members had moved out of the house, too afraid to live there any longer.

HOT AND COLD RUNNING GHOSTS

Another strange symptom of poltergeist activity is a sudden change in room temperature. During both a haunting and poltergeist activity a room will often become much colder, as if a window or door were suddenly open to a draft of frigid air. Some researchers have pointed out that hauntings and poltergeist activity both seem to draw energy from the surroundings in order to manifest themselves, thus causing a feeling of coldness in a place, as if the spirit were draining energy from the place or a person.

When studying paranormal events, investigators always come across notable exceptions to every rule. Alan Gauld and Tony Cornell are two British parapsychologists who have made careful studies of poltergeist events reported around the world. In one interesting case they classify as a "minor haunting," witnesses felt considerably warmer instead of colder in the presence of the poltergeist.

The case took place in 1971 and 1972 and involved Mr. and Mrs. J. and their four children. Mr. and Mrs. J. were both teachers at a technical college and the investigators considered them to be reliable and sincere witnesses. Mr. J. noted in his diary the strange events in his new house, which began even before the family moved in. In his own words, here is a description of one encounter with a poltergeist:

The first inexplicable phenomenon took place when I was decorating upstairs. My father was with me on the landing. For no apparent reason I suddenly felt hot all over for a few seconds. I moved further along the landing in the course of my work and felt very hot again. Within a few seconds my temperature went back to normal . . . It seemed as though there were a moving column of hot air—15 to 20 degrees warmer than the surrounding air. It caught up with me as I was working and moved on past me. . . . It moved at a slow walking pace clockwise around

41

the perimeter of the landing . . . I would have said it was about the thickness of a man's body. I did not check the height.

Mr. J.'s father also tracked the strange column of warm air for a time. Both men would have probably forgotten about the minor incident if other oddities had not begun to occur in the new house almost as soon as the family moved in. There were unexplainable sounds, floating teaspoons, the frequent sound of a trunk being dragged across the top landing, and the sound of a drawer in a bedroom chest opening and closing quickly.

The family was scared and confused, but none of the events had been quite frightening enough to chase them out of their new home.

One night, when Mrs. J.'s sister came to visit with her five children, all the children asked for permission to sleep out in the backyard in tents. The next morning, the girls who were ages nine and six rushed in to their parents, saying they had seen a burglar in the house during the night.

Mr. J.'s daughter Jill told investigators that she and her cousin woke up early and decided to peek in the house to see what time it was. They looked through the window in the parlor and saw a man standing by the mantelpiece. At first she described him as leaning with his elbow on either side of the clock on the mantelpiece.

But later she told investigators that he was holding the mantelpiece clock in his hands. The man was dressed in a suit and the girls said they saw him turn and disappear near a bookcase.

Jill thought it was about half past five in the morning when they had seen the figure by the mantelpiece. When Mr. J. checked the clock on the mantelpiece, he was shocked to find it had permanently stopped, the hands showing the time of fifteen minutes past three. Clocks permanently stopped in the presence of apparitions or a poltergeist is another strange side-effect often reported.

Was the apparition of the man by the fireplace connected in some way to the column of warm air? Investigators could not say. Like many other ghost stories, the bizarre events that happened in this household did not seem to have much meaning or reason.

The disturbances ended in November 1972, as abruptly as they had begun. The paranormal events that plagued Mr. and Mrs. J. and their family could not be considered strictly poltergeist phenomenon, since an apparition was sighted by the girls. But as you will see, in many cases hauntings and poltergeist events do seem to overlap, or to combine elements of both types of ghosts.

FIRES AND FLOODS

Poltergeists don't always limit their mischief to moving objects or smashing crockery. There

have been a few rarer cases when poltergeists caused small fires to break out around a house, or caused small puddles of water to appear on the floor or other surfaces. Sometimes the amount of water was much more than a puddle or two, even enough to cause a sizable flood. Other liquids, like beer or milk, have also been reported. When water or another liquid appears, it is sometimes the only evidence of a poltergeist, causing some investigators to set aside these reports in a special category of "water poltergeist."

In a very unusual case investigated by Gauld and Cornell, the investigators in the Mr. and Mrs. J. case, a home was disturbed by both fires and floods of water. The house was located in a small village near Bath, England. The investigators noted that the house was built "on stony ground on top of a hill; not a likely site for an underground stream . . . or for the accumulation of underground water."

The family, Mr. and Mrs. W. and three of their four children, was first disturbed by strange events in March of 1963. Most of the events happened in the daytime, while Mr. W. was at work and the children were in school, leaving Mrs. W. to put up with most of the poltergeist activity. When A. D. Cornell first visited the house in September to investigate, he found Mrs. W. exhausted from the weird events in her household. As he walked toward the

house, he saw Mrs. W. ironing with her ironing board set up a few feet outside the front door. She explained that it was difficult to get any work done inside because of the sudden floods and outbreaks of fire.

The first flood had occurred in March. Large quantities of water had poured down from the living room ceiling. It looked as if a pipe in the ceiling had burst—a natural enough explanation, it would seem. Yet soon after the pipe in the ceiling was repaired, a pool of water began to appear on the living room floor. When a builder was called in to find the cause, he could not find any leaks in the pipes or the foundation.

Over the next few months, water would frequently overflow from the home's water tank, located in a closet over the hall. Plumbers and the heating experts sent by the local housing council came to the home again and again, but could not find any cause for the floods. The tank and several other parts of the building's plumbing and heating system were replaced. In fact, several tanks of different designs and metals were installed during the next months.

But it seemed that as soon as the house was empty, or the system left unobserved, there would be another flood. Baffled, the heating and plumbing experts decided to leave standing buckets of water at different locations around the house and found that these too (even though

they were not connected to any water pipes) overflowed and caused small floods when no one was watching.

One night, Mrs. W. came home from playing bingo to find that the water tank had edged itself away from the wall. The pipes connecting it to the wall were found scattered on the floor. The tank was pushed back into place. But once again, when nobody was home a neighbor heard sounds from the house. Later, when the W. family called in the plumbing expert, he found that the tank had somehow moved out of the closet. It finally moved itself down the hall and tumbled down the stairs.

The first fire Mrs. W. witnessed was an armchair in flames. Other fires were smaller and often mainly smoke. For example, Mrs. W. sometimes found balls of newspaper smoldering in the corners of the house. In November she came home and discovered that both a rug and part of the dining room table were scorched, but not in flames. The next day she came in and found the tablecloth and wallpaper scorched. About two weeks later she returned home during the day and found the living room curtains in flames. Mrs. W. didn't like to leave the house because she was afraid of what she would find when she came back.

In addition to the floods and fires in the W. family home, some small objects were found in odd places and once Mrs. W. saw her hairbrush

glide several feet across the bedroom. The unexplainable events faded out and ended around November. Gauld and Cornell have called this case "the most expert account of 'water poltergeist' yet published."

POLTERGEIST DESTRUCTION

Poltergeists have been known to mess up rooms or houses by rumpling bedclothes, cutting or tearing clothes, and even tying clothes or curtains in knots. Sometimes objects in a room are arranged in patterns or strange smells emerge from nowhere, ranging from the scent of roses to odors so foul that people are left gasping for air.

The list of all poltergeist mischief ever witnessed would be a long one. In a book called *This House Is Haunted,* Guy Playfair, a famous psychic researcher, lists nineteen symptoms of poltergeist disturbances and the likely order of their appearance. Based on his investigations of poltergeists, it seemed to Playfair that there was a predictable order to the activity. For instance, poltergeists will first make themselves known with noises, usually a tapping or knocking in a wall. Flying crockery, moving furniture, or spontaneous fires or floods will usually come later.

Like the poltergeist that plagued Ernest Rivers, most cases last for only a few weeks. But as seen in the cases of the J. and W. families, some

have been known to persist for many months, even a year or longer.

THE SAUCHIE POLTERGEIST

Except for Ernest Rivers, in the cases we have looked at so far the poltergeist disturbances have not been clearly focused on one member of a household. Many researchers feel, however, that poltergeists in a household always act with some specific focus or agent. The events may not always be directed at that person (for instance, the way the pepper shaker and other objects flew at Ernest Rivers), but when that person is not present the disturbances usually fade out.

Very often an unhappy teenager or adolescent is the focus of poltergeist activity. In centuries past—and even today—when poltergeist activity erupts in a household and focuses on a young girl or boy, some people believe that the child is being possessed or taken over by evil spirits. Priests and other religious figures are brought to the house to exorcise, or chase out, the "demons." The famous book and film *The Exorcist* was a dramatization of this situation.

Parapsychologists point out that in the case of poltergeist disturbances, exorcism will rarely end the phenomenon. Sometimes it even seems to stir things up and make the activity more intense.

When poltergeist events began to focus on

eleven-year-old Virginia Campbell, some thought she was indeed possessed by evil spirits and called the Reverend T. Lund to the house.

Virginia was brought up on a farm in County Donegal, Ireland. She had few companions to play with except for her dog Toby and a friend named Anna. When her father sold his share of the farm, the family had to live apart for a while. Virginia and her mother went to Scotland. While her mother worked in a nearby town, Virginia was sent to live with her older brother Thomas, who was married and had two children close to Virginia's age.

Virginia's brother and his family lived in the town of Sauchie in Clackmannshire, Scotland. Virginia came to stay with them about mid-October. She had been there about a month when the poltergeist activity began.

As in most poltergeist cases, the disturbances began slowly and were not very overwhelming. One night in late November, the sound of a bouncing ball was heard in Virginia's bedroom and on the stairs, but no cause could be found. The next day, as Virginia had tea with her older brother and his wife, a very large piece of furniture began to move away from the wall, then moved back.

That night when sounds started again the disturbances became more obvious. There were loud knocks heard in the bedroom Virginia shared with her brother's daughter Margaret,

Copy 1

EAST HIGH
Learning Resource Center

who was nine years old. The noises were so loud that a neighbor called the Reverend T. W. Lund, the Church of Scotland minister of Sauchie. He was a witness to many odd events that night and afterward. Because of his position as clergyman, investigators consider him to be a reliable witness.

Among the events Reverend Lund reported were loud knockings while Virginia was in bed with her feet tucked under the bedclothes and no part of her body touching the bedframe. He also saw a large, full linen chest that was standing near the bed rock, raise up, move along the side of the bed for about two feet, then move back.

Two nights later, the reverend visited again and saw other strange sights. There were more raps and knockings and Virginia's pillow turned under her head. A doctor named Dr. W. H. Nisbet, along with another minister and a medical professional, were called in by Reverend Lund. These men, the family members, and other witnesses heard a sawing sound and more knocking, and also observed a strange rippling motion move across Virginia's pillow.

The doctors could not find anything physically wrong with Virginia, so the next day she went to school. Miss Margaret Stewart, Virginia's teacher, was looking out at the children during a period of silent reading and saw Virginia trying to press down the lid of her

desk, which popped up several times, opening itself about halfway. Miss Stewart could see quite clearly that the girl was not pushing the lid up herself. A few moments later, Miss Stewart saw the desk behind Virginia float up into the air about an inch off the floor, then slowly float down again. Checking the area around the desk, Miss Stewart was sure that no strings had been attached to it.

That night, the same strange events were witnessed in Virginia's bedroom by Dr. Nisbet—the knocks, the moving linen chest (which also opened and closed its lid a few times), the rotating pillow, and the rippling bed covers. Two nights later, Dr. Nisbet visited with his partner, Dr. Logan, who brought along his dog. Virginia liked the dog very much and said it reminded her of her dog, Toby. A little while later, Virginia went into a trance. She called for her dog and at one point screamed loudly, tossing and striking her fists in the air. Then she became calmer and fell asleep.

The next week, Virginia went to school on Monday morning as usual. While she was standing near Miss Stewart at the teacher's table, a pointer began to vibrate and move across the table. Miss Stewart reached down to touch the table and the table swung around counterclockwise. Virginia became scared and started to cry, afraid that Miss Stewart thought she was playing a trick. But Miss Stewart did not blame

her and could see that she had not been touching the pointer or the table.

That afternoon, Virginia was sent to stay with another relative in a nearby town. The change in location, however, did not bring an end to the poltergeist activity surrounding her. Dr. Nisbet and Dr. Logan visited her in her new home and observed some of the same events.

THE POLTERGEIST IS ASKED TO GO

On December 1, a day after Virginia returned to her brother's house, Dr. Nisbet, Dr. Logan, and Reverend Lund visited the house in the evening. Dr. Nisbet and Dr. Logan brought a tape recorder and successfully recorded sounds of sawing and rapping. They also brought a motion picture camera, but did not get a clear image on film of the blanket rippling. During their visit, Virginia entered another trance-like state, speaking almost hysterically for about an hour.

Late that night, at about eleven o'clock, the Reverend Lund and two other ministers performed a religious service. During the service, several knocks were heard. It is often observed that religious intervention makes the activity worse. But the events were much less frequent after that night. As in other poltergeist activity, the events became gradually less frequent, until they stopped altogether in about March.

CHAPTER FIVE:
MORE POWERFUL
POLTERGEISTS

As we have seen, poltergeists are mischief makers and although their activity can seem dangerous, their antics usually toe the line just this side of causing any serious harm or injury. Some typical physical sensations caused by poltergeists are a lot like the "rough play" of children in a schoolyard. A victim of a poltergeist may have the sensation of being pinched, bitten, scratched, pushed, or restrained by some unseen force.

However, poltergeists are not always stirring up trouble "just for fun." In some recorded cases, the poltergeist's wrath is much more violent and malicious. Guy Playfair recounts a Brazilian case involving a young girl who was

so distraught over the poltergeist activity that she committed suicide.

THE CASE OF THE "BELL WITCH"

The poltergeist known as the Bell Witch is another of the rare recorded cases when poltergeist events caused a person's death. The spirit descended upon the unfortunate family of John Bell, who lived in Robertson County, Tennessee. John Bell and his wife Lucy had nine children. The strange disturbances began around their household in 1817 and persisted for about three years.

The "witch," as the entity came to be known, first made itself known with scratching and tapping sounds, some that sounded as if they were made by animals. Covers flew off the children's beds at night and weird sounds like someone being choked or strangled were heard. As noted in other cases, the repertoire of the Bell Witch included stone throwing and overturned furniture. The children sometimes felt their heads pulled so hard that they screamed.

Betsy, the Bells' twelve-year-old daughter, seemed to be the agent or poltergeist focus. Much of the spirit's vicious energy was directed at her, and things seemed to happen most when she was in the house. When Betsy was sent to stay with a neighbor, things calmed down in the house, but she continued to feel stinging slaps and scratches.

THE BELL WITCH SPEAKS

After over a year had passed, the spirit manifested a voice. The "witch" now seemed more interested in John Bell than Betsy, and often promised that "old Jack Bell" would be tortured for the rest of his days. By this time Betsy had begun having fainting spells. Her father was often in pain from a swollen tongue and stiff jaw. The unexplainable ailment often made it difficult for him to eat.

Poltergeists that manifest a voice are rare, as mentioned before. The Bell Witch was an even more unique case because it seemed to speak at different times in more than one voice. One voice identified itself as "a spirit who was once very happy, but [had] been disturbed and [is] now unhappy." Another time it said it was an Indian, and another time, a witch.

All of the Bell Witch's activity was not vindictive, however. Once on Betsy's birthday, the witch's voice was heard to say it was sending the girl a surprise. Suddenly, a basket of oranges, bananas, and other fruit appeared from out of nowhere—quite a rare delicacy in the Tennessee countryside over a century ago.

POISONED BY A POLTERGEIST

The visit of the Bell Witch had a sad ending. As the voice had promised, John Bell's suffering continued. He was often so sick he had to be in

bed. The muscles in his face sometimes jerked and contorted and his body went into convulsive spasms. On December 20, 1820, he went into a coma-like state and could not be revived.

A strange bottle of medicine was found in a cupboard. The "witch" voice claimed she had given John Bell a dose of the liquid the night before and promised it would kill him. Reportedly, a doctor arrived and tested the medicine on a cat. The cat died moments later. When John Bell died the next day, it is reported that the witch's screams of triumph sounded throughout the unhappy house.

In 1846, Richard Bell, who had been seven when the poltergeist first began to torment his family, wrote a full account of the story. He said that after the death of John Bell, the spirit made contact with the family a few more times, but without any significant message or event. The "witch" did promise to return in one hundred and seven years to haunt a descendant. But in 1935 no member of the family reported a return of the Bell Witch.

IS THIS ANY PLACE FOR A POLTERGEIST?

So far we have looked at cases of poltergeists who have invaded unsuspecting households. But poltergeists have been known to visit places other than family homes. A poltergeist-like spirit was reported in a tea room called the Eastwind Restaurant, located in the town of

Wiscasset, Maine. Dorothy F. Apgar, who owns and runs the restaurant, reported the poltergeist to psychic researcher Susy Smith in the early 1960s. The restaurant was originally a house and was built around 1800. The building had also held the town's first apothecary shop (an old-fashioned version of a drugstore).

The haunting entity is known as Lydia or Mother Dana. She was a relative or wife of the man who had built the house, Charles Dana. Lydia's poltergeist pranks only go on in the daytime. She overturns teapots, tips over trays, and spills the food from dishes as waitresses hurry to tables with their orders. Latched doors open by themselves and chairs have been known to move out from under tables, untouched by human hands.

The restaurant owner, Dorothy Apgar, claims to be the focus of the spirit's energies—which have often pushed her down flights of stairs. Because of these falls, Dorothy has had several broken bones. But she refuses any offers to have the poltergeist Lydia turned out. In her book *Haunted Houses for the Millions*, Smith quotes Dorothy Apgar as saying, "I'm going to keep her. I'll win her over with love."

SMASHED SOUVENIRS OF SUNNY FLORIDA

Perhaps one of the most peculiar settings for a poltergeist report is the case of a spirit entity

active in a novelty and souvenir company in Miami, Florida.

Strange events in a souvenir company called Tropicana Arts began about mid-December in 1966. Susy Smith brought the case to the attention of two well-known parapsychologists, Mr. W. G. Roll, Director of the Physical Foundation in Durham, North Carolina, and Professor J. G. Pratt of the University of Virginia. Along with Ms. Smith, Pratt and Roll had the chance to visit the Tropicana Arts Company and study the poltergeist activity firsthand. Not only was the Miami poltergeist found in one of the most unique settings, it is also probably one of the best-observed and -documented cases to date.

The activity happened only in the company warehouse, which was a large rectangular-shaped room filled with shelves that ran along the walls and down the middle of the room. On the shelves, various souvenirs sold by the company were stored in boxes or loosely wrapped. The items were a veritable poltergeist picnic and included mugs, glasses, jars, bottles, and many other breakable objects.

The main focus or agent of the events was a young man who worked in the warehouse named Julio Vasquez. Some events also seemed to be focused on a young woman who painted some of the souvenirs.

It was reported that at times objects flew off the shelves "as fast as they could be picked up

or swept up." Curiously, although Julio seemed to be the focus of the events in the warehouse the poltergeist activity did not continue when he was at home. After a lot of stock was broken and damaged, the police were finally called. Four police officers gathered together all the people who worked in the warehouse, but the sound of smashing glass still continued to be heard.

The company owners were remarkably tolerant of the situation and did not fire Julio, or even ask him to remain at home. Unlike most other cases, the poltergeist activity did not follow Julio to his home. As in other cases, the events gradually faded out and the warehouse returned to normal. Why they began in the first place continues to remain a mystery.

WHO—OR WHAT—ARE THEY?

There are several different explanations for poltergeist disturbances. One explanation says that the mischievous activity is caused by spirits of deceased persons that are drawing their energy from the focus or poltergeist agent. Others believe that many poltergeists may be a form of nonhuman intelligence or a nonhuman entity.

A Frenchman named Leon Rivail, who lived in Paris during the mid-nineteenth century, advanced this second poltergeist theory. Rivail was a teacher and self-styled philosopher who traveled around giving lectures on many topics,

such as chemistry and astronomy. Rivail became curious about psychic events, particularly seances, which were quite popular at the time in both Europe and America. With the help of two young women who were mediums, Rivail believed that he had received important and detailed information from the spirit world about poltergeists and many other related subjects.

The spirits instructed Rivail to publish this information in a book. They told him the title, *The Spirits' Book,* and even told him to take a new name, Allen Kardec. The book was published in 1856 and was quite popular.

According to Kardec, the universe is filled with many kinds of spirits, or intelligent energy that is not contained in a physical body. Human beings are bodies united with a spirit. Kardec said that human beings can improve themselves during their lifetime, and after their physical body dies their spirit can return in another body. This notion is known as reincarnation and is a widely held belief of many Eastern religions, such as Buddhism or Hinduism.

In between various lives, a spirit may be floating around without a body, Kardec explained. Some of these spirits are mischief makers and cause poltergeist effects. However, Kardec believed that only a few poltergeist cases are caused by the spirits of dead people. There are many types of spirits, and most poltergeist events are caused by a different kind.

These non-human spirits are thought by some to be a lower form of spirit life and sometimes more malicious or uncontrollable. Perhaps that notion is in some ways a bit eerier than thinking of poltergeists as the spirits of deceased persons.

CHAPTER SIX: LONG-DISTANCE CALLS— CONTACTING THE SPIRIT WORLD

The people we've read about who have seen ghosts or had their households turned upside down by poltergeists certainly had not expected these uninvited houseguests.

But not all spirits arrive uninvited. As mentioned before, some people believe that you can contact and communicate with the spirit world easily. This is a belief of spiritualists. Modern spiritualists believe that a soul or spirit survives when the body dies, and that the spirits of the dead can communicate with the living. But not everyone can speak to spirits. Spiritualists (and others) believe that only people with special powers that enable them to see, hear, and feel things others cannot have the ability to contact

the spirit world. These extra-sensitive people are called mediums or psychics.

RAPS AND KNOCKS IN HYDESVILLE, NEW YORK

The history of modern spiritualism began in 1848 in a farmhouse in Hydesville, New York. The Fox family, who lived in the farmhouse, could hardly get a good night of sleep during the month of March because of the loud rapping and knocking noises that would start up at night. The two younger girls in the family, ten-year-old Margaret and seven-year-old Kate, started clapping and snapping their fingers one night in answer to the noises. Quite amazingly, the sounds echoed the exact number of the snaps. The girls were terrified and their father tried to figure out some logical reason for the sounds. Nobody knew what was making the sounds, but the strange force that answered seemed to have some intelligence.

A neighbor who came over to hear the sounds decided to ask the rapping force some questions. The force replied with one rap for "yes" and two for "no." Using a code for the letters of the alphabet, the force later identified itself as the spirit of a man named Charles B. Rosma. Charles Rosma's spirit said he had been a peddler and had been murdered in the house five years before.

After that, the spirit manifest itself with some of the typical features of hauntings that we have

read about—there were also sounds of a death struggle, gurgling, and sounds of a body being dragged across the floors.

The police investigated the spirit's story, but could find no record of a peddler named Charles Rosma. However, in 1904 a wall in the yard a few feet from the cellar was being repaired. Digging near the cellar, the workman found a man's skeleton and a peddler's tin box buried in the yard. Was it Charles Rosma's remains, which would substantiate the spirit's claims? It is impossible to know for sure.

"THE DAWNING OF A NEW ERA"

For several months after the spirit's first communication with the Fox family, the haunting became worse and worse. The family decided to communicate once more with the spirit force that was causing them so much trouble. They called out the letters of the alphabet and then listened for the spirit's raps at a certain letter. Slowly but surely, a message was spelled out. Leah Fox served as the medium or psychic and led the communication. The first message Leah received began with the words "Dear friends, you must proclaim this truth to the world. This is the dawning of a new era; you must not try to conceal it any longer. When you do your duty God will protect you and good spirits will watch over you."

On November 14, 1849, the Fox sisters pub-

licly demonstrated their ability to contact spirits for a small group of people assembled in the Corinthian Hall in the city of Rochester, New York. The gathering is considered the first meeting of the Spiritualist Movement.

Some citizens were outraged at the Fox sisters' claims. Several groups investigated the Fox sisters, but they could not find any evidence that the young women were causing the rapping sounds themselves. Even when the Fox sisters were standing on pillows and a handkerchief tied the bottom of their dresses tightly around their ankles (to make any leg movement beneath their dresses visible), nobody could prove that young women were making the sounds.

Within six months after the first meeting of the Spiritualist Movement, the three Fox sisters—Leah, Margaret, and Kate—were all professional mediums who charged admission to their seances, which they called "sittings."

CALLING SPIRITS—A PARTY GAME, OR SERIOUS BUSINESS?

The most common method of holding a seance is for a small group of people to gather around a table and call upon the spirits to communicate with them. Usually, the room is dark and the group will hold hands or put their hands on the table with their fingertips spread wide so that each person is touching his neighbors'. A spirit medium or psychic is usually

present to lead the group and receive the spirits' messages.

At a seance or sitting, the spirits announce their presence by causing the table to shake or knock against the floor. Sometimes, other knocks will be heard or the table will turn, vibrate, rise up in the air, or balance on two legs.

In the 1850s, soon after the Fox sisters and the events at Hydesville became widely known, the Spiritualist Movement swept through America and Europe. To some, calling on spirits was only an amusing pastime—a parlor game to play with guests at a dinner party. But others were very serious about seances and believed that psychics really could contact the spirit world.

As interest in spiritualism grew, many mediums became famous for their amazing feats. Florence Cook, Leonore Piper, Mrs. Samuel Guppy, Eusapia Palladine, and Daniel Dunglas Home, a few of the best-known psychics at this time, were known in America, England, and Europe.

There are many stories of the astounding sights and events that occurred at seances conducted by these mediums and others. In addition to table shaking and knocking sounds, it was common for those at a seance to report that they saw hands or even an entire spirit-form materialize. Sometimes the medium would lev-

itate (lift out of the chair) or even float around the room.

THE AMAZING FEATS OF D. D. HOME

Daniel Dunglas Home was one of the most famous mediums of his day. Home was born in Scotland in 1833 and raised in America by his aunt. As a child he reported seeing visions, first of a childhood friend, and later, a vision predicting his mother's death. As his psychic abilities became more obvious, his aunt thought Home was possessed by demons. She called several ministers from different churches to perform exorcism on her nephew, but Home's psychic powers continued to manifest.

When his aunt eventually forced him to leave her house, Home moved to Europe. He was handsome, charming, and quite entertaining. He attracted friends quickly, especially wealthy friends, and many people were fascinated by his psychic talents. Home never accepted money for his performances, but lived quite comfortably on the hospitality of his rich and famous patrons.

His fascinated audiences ranged from scientists to royalty and included Elizabeth Barrett Browning and Emperor Napoleon III of France. Throughout his life, Home astounded hundreds of witnesses with his remarkable feats. While Home was in a trance during a seance, furniture might float in the air, rising all

the way to the ceiling. The sound of trumpets or tambourines might fill the room. Sounds of birds, splashing water, or spirit voices were also heard. According to some reports, dead people would materialize and talk to the seance group, looking quite solid and real. Sometimes a pair of phantom hands would appear, which were quite a shocking sight.

There is one famous report that Home defied gravity by floating through an open window three stories above the ground and reentered the house through another window on the same floor. The famous levitation took place in a London townhouse on December 13, 1868, in the presence of three witnesses. The witnesses claimed that Home went into a trance, then went to the next room. They heard the window in that room open. A few seconds later, they saw Home floating upright outside the window of their room.

The house had no ledge around the window, nor was there any obvious or even logical way Home could have managed to get from one window to the other by maneuvering on the outside of the building. The witnesses reported that Home opened the window and floated in, laughing at the shocked look on everyone's face.

Another astounding physical feat by D. D. Home was an ability to grow taller during a seance, which he said was due to spirit influence.

Home would say that the spirit he had contacted was tall and strong, then it would appear to those present at the seance that Home himself grew—as much as six to eight inches.

Home claimed that all his strange psychic powers came through the spirit world. Home was investigated by several scientists and others who did not believe in spiritualism or psychic phenomenon. Although Home did not always produce spectacular events at seances, he was never discovered to be faking any phenomenon.

Home and other famous mediums of this era were studied very closely by prominent scientists. In the next chapter, we will take a closer look at past and present scientific investigations of mediums and psychic phenomenon.

MESSAGES FROM THE OTHER SIDE

Toward the end of the nineteenth century, the activities of mediums during seances began to change a great deal from D. D. Home's techniques. The many spectacular physical feats—such as pianos rising in the air, knocking sounds, music, and materialization of spirit hands or figures—occurred less and less. During a seance, mediums instead focused on relaying spoken or written messages from the spirits.

Some of these messages came through a process called automatic writing, as well as through a device called a ouija board. To receive a message through automatic writing, a medium will

usually balance a pencil or pen against their fingers, barely touching it. The pencil will begin to move as the spirit force controls the words that are written out. The ouija board gets its name from the French and German words for "yes" (*oui* and *ja*). It is a board with the alphabet and the words *yes* and *no* written on it. To receive a message from spirits with a ouija board, one or more persons will lightly rest their fingertips on a pointer that will glide across the board (guided by the spirits who are answering) to spell out a message.

In another seance method that uses the letters of the alphabet, letter cards are spread out on a table in a circle. Resting their fingertips on the edge of an overturned wineglass, the seance group (called sitters) will find that the glass will move from letter to letter, spelling out a message.

Calling on spirits with a ouija board or by other means is not recommended to everyone, however. In fact, it can sometimes produce unwanted and even frightening results. It has been reported that people who are merely curious about such matters and stage a seance or play with a ouija board for fun can summon up unwanted and malicious spirits.

During a seance with a professional medium, a ouija board or even automatic writing is not usually used. Instead, the medium goes into a trance state. The psychic might look and act as

if they are hypnotized, or as if they are awake, yet dreaming. The medium's voice, posture, and facial expression will often undergo dramatic transformations. Once in a trance, the medium will relay the spirit messages vocally.

Most mediums do not claim to speak directly with spirits, but say that they communicate through a spirit-guide or control, which they contact first. The spirit-guide then finds other spirits, communicates with them, and gives their messages to the medium. Sometimes a medium's special spirit-guide will identify itself as a person the medium knew when the spirit was alive.

The spoken or written messages that began to come through mediums in the late nineteenth and early twentieth century contained precise, substantial information. Sometimes the information was very personal, and perhaps even told a secret between the sitter (the person asking the questions) and a person who had died. The ability to convey such personal messages from the dead often shocked even those who believed in a medium's psychic powers.

LEONORE PIPER: THE WORLD'S GREATEST TRANCE MEDIUM

Leonore Piper was considered by some to be the greatest trance medium who ever lived. She was certainly one of the most thoroughly observed and investigated. William James the

American philosopher and psychologist, Sir
Oliver Lodge, a prominent physicist, Dr. Richard Hodgson, who had studied and lectured on
law at Cambridge University but devoted his
life to psychical research, and Professor George
Hervey Hyslop, professor of logic and ethics at
Columbia University, were among the distinguished scientists and scholars who studied
Mrs. Piper's psychic powers. At first, Hodgson
did not believe mediums could communicate
with a spirit world. But after observing Mrs.
Piper, he became so fascinated by her abilities
that he virtually dedicated his life to studying
her.

Mrs. Piper is considered one of the most convincing examples of mediumship because she
was studied for such a long period of time and
because her sittings were performed under scientific controls employed by Hodgson and
other investigators.

Professor James observed Mrs. Piper during
twelve seances and studied the accounts of
twenty-four sitters whom he had sent to her. In
1886 he reported these findings in a scientific
journal: "I now believe her to be in possession
of a power as yet unexplained." Although James
was thoroughly convinced of Mrs. Piper's psychic abilities, he readily confessed that he could
not explain them.

Mrs. Piper began her career as a medium in
1884, shortly after the birth of her first daugh-

ter. While attending a meeting held by a medium named J. R. Cocke, Mrs. Piper fell into a
trance. She scribbled a message on a piece of
paper and gave it to a man at the meeting named
Judge Frost. Judge Frost, who was a spiritualist,
was astounded when he read the note. He an-
nounced that Mrs. Piper had received a message
from his dead son. When Mrs. Piper gave Judge
Frost the message, he considered it the most
significant proof of the existence of a spirit
realm he had ever seen.

Soon after that experience, Mrs. Piper began
to give sittings for others. Eventually, she began
to charge fees for putting people in touch with
their dead loved ones. She and her family lived
near Boston, Massachusetts, in a neighborhood
known as Arlington Heights.

Mrs. Piper had many spirit-guides. As mentioned before, a spirit-guide acts as an interpre-
tor for the psychic, relaying messages from
other spirits. Some of Mrs. Piper's were famous, like the poet Henry Wadsworth Longfel-
low and the composer Johann Sebastian Bach.
Her main spirit-guide, however, identified himself as Dr. Phinuit, the spirit of a French phy-
sician who had lived in Metz, France, and died
many years before.

When Mrs. Piper prepared to go into a trance
to contact Dr. Phinuit, she would first relax in
a comfortable chair and breathe deeply. She
would hold the patron's or sitter's hands

tightly. Sometimes trembling, her posture and facial expression and gestures would gradually become more masculine. When she spoke, her voice was harsher, deeper, and had a French accent.

Sometimes Dr. Phinuit, speaking through Mrs. Piper, would amaze sitters by calling out names of family members and sounding familiar with their activities and even their ailments. He told of forgotten or secret incidents that the sitters acknowledged were true. Other times, however, it seemed that the medium was fishing for information by asking questions (Who is George? Do you know a Margaret or a Martha? Is the letter N significant to you?) rather than telling the sitter information.

Sometimes Dr. Phinuit would be completely wrong. For example, when visited by Sir Oliver Lodge (who was then professor of physics at University College in Liverpool), Dr. Phinuit told Lodge that one of his sons had worms, which was correct. However, when Dr. Phinuit was asked to name the boy's special interest, he said, "natural things; is musical." However, this was not true. Lodge later noted that the boy was very interested in architecture and drew pictures or read books about buildings whenever he had time. He wasn't much interested in nature, or music.

But some scientists who studied psychics did not believe that spirit-guides had to give correct

information all the time in order to prove their existence. They considered that since it came through the medium and whatever unknown obstacles that might exist, the information could get blurred. In addition, they theorized, perhaps spirits do not have a clear memory of life on earth once they have arrived in the after-world.

Many scientists visited Mrs. Piper and participated in what was known as a "controlled sitting." At this type of sitting the visitors were known by the scientist studying the medium (usually Dr. Hodgson). The sitters were introduced to Mrs. Piper under false names and every effort was made to keep Mrs. Piper from knowing even the slightest bit of information about them. Sometimes they would be masked and would not utter a word to her, only shake their head "yes" or "no" in reply to questions. In this way, Hodgson attempted to be sure that Mrs. Piper's only knowledge of the visitors came through her spirit contacts.

After observing her meetings with fifty people, he wrote, "Most of these persons were told facts through the trance utterance which they felt sure could not have become known to Mrs. Piper by ordinary means." Hodgson even went to the trouble of having private detectives follow Mrs. Piper for three weeks to find out if she or her husband was secretly collecting information on people who visited her.

THE WORDS IN THE RINGS

As already mentioned, some who visited Mrs. Piper came away disappointed or unconvinced that she had any special power. Others, however, were astounded. One of the most famous stories about Mrs. Piper involved a Professor Herbert Nichols, who lectured at Harvard and was sent to Mrs. Piper by Professor William James.

While visiting Mrs. Piper, Nichols presented the medium with a special test of her abilities. His mother had once given him a ring with the first word of his favorite proverb engraved in it and he had given her a similar ring with the first word of her favorite proverb engraved in it as well. He had lost his ring, but after his mother's death, he had come into possession of her ring. Holding his mother's ring in his hand, he concentrated on the inscription and asked Mrs. Piper, "What is written in Mamma's ring?" Mrs. Piper responded by quickly writing something down on a piece of paper. Nichols was amazed when he read it. It was not the word written on the ring in his hand, but the word written on the ring he had lost so long ago.

Nichols considered this incident and other very personal information he heard from the medium to be great proof of Mrs. Piper's psychic powers. He wrote to James, "She is no fraud. . . . She is the greatest marvel I have ever met. I am now wholly convinced."

LEONORE PIPER AND THE SPIRIT OF GEORGE PELLEW

In later years, Leonore Piper was in contact with other spirit-guides besides Dr. Phinuit. One was the spirit of George Pellew, who had died in New York City in February 1892, at the age of thirty-two from injuries he sustained when he fell off a horse. Pellew had studied law at Harvard University, but had given up law in order to write. He wrote under the name of George Pelham. His interest in philosophy and other diverse topics included psychical research. He had once attended one of Mrs. Piper's seances under a false name.

Pellew was skeptical of mediums and did not believe that the soul survived death or that spirits of the dead could communicate with the living. He had told friends, including Professor Hodgson, that if he could return as a spirit he would, and that he would "make things lively."

George Pellew's spirit did not waste much time making good on his promise. It was about a month after his death that George Pellew's voice first came through Mrs. Piper. A friend of Pellew's was at the seance and had been introduced to Mrs. Piper under a false name. When he gave Mrs. Piper a stud from his shirt, the medium said in a voice that sounded much like Pellew's, "That's mine . . . I sent that to you." The friend asked, "When?" and George Pellew's spirit replied, "Before I came here."

Meaning, before he arrived in the afterworld. This was not entirely true, but close enough to give those involved a chill. The shirt stud had been Pellew's but had been given to the friend by Pellew's father after his death.

George Pellew's spirit continued to communicate through Mrs. Piper, sometimes through the process of automatic writing. The spirit would take control of Mrs. Piper's right hand as she wrote with a pencil on a pad, and in this way responded to questions of sitters. Professor Hodgson tested the spirit of George Pellew by bringing sitters to Mrs. Piper who had known Pellew when he was alive. These sitters were introduced under false names. Pellew's spirit recognized all those he had known during his lifetime and never claimed to know anyone he had not met.

During the early years of observing Mrs. Piper, Professor Hodgson did not believe that her information came from the spirit world. But after these experiences with Pellew's spirit, he believed that spirits of the dead could indeed communicate with the living through a medium.

After Hodgson's death in 1905, the study of Mrs. Piper's psychic powers was continued by Dr. Hyslop of Columbia University. A few days after Dr. Hyslop began sittings with Mrs. Piper, the spirit of Hodgson began communi-

cating through the medium and acting as Mrs. Piper's new spirit-guide. Hyslop was at first skeptical of Mrs. Piper, but after twelve sittings he truly felt he had been conversing with "my father, my brother, my uncles . . ." through Mrs. Piper and the spirit of Hodgson.

Since Mrs. Piper could communicate information known only to the dead person and the sitter, many investigators believed that she provided convincing evidence of the spirit's survival and of a medium's ability to communicate with a spirit world.

EILEEN GARRETT AND THE CRASH OF AIRSHIP R101

Like Leonore Piper, Eileen Garrett was a famous American medium who was closely studied by psychical researchers. She also assisted in investigations of hauntings, as we saw earlier in the case of the Green Man of Ash Manor. Eileen Garrett founded the Parapsychology Foundation in New York and wrote several books on parapsychology. Throughout her lifetime, she encouraged the scientific and systematically controlled study of paranormal events.

The most extraordinary seance Mrs. Garrett ever performed occurred on October 7, 1930. It took place at the National Laboratory of Psychical Research in London, England. The research center had been set up in 1926 by Harry Price, a famous investigator of psychic events. In addition to Price and Garrett, Price's secre-

tary and a reporter, Ian D. Coster, were present.

The purpose of the seance had been to contact the spirit of the author Sir Arthur Conan Doyle. Sir Conan Doyle was a writer, famous for creating the character Sherlock Holmes. He believed very strongly in the survival of the spirit. Sir Conan Doyle had recently died, and Price hoped to contact his spirit through the mediumship of Eileen Garrett.

The seance began and Mrs. Garrett went into a trance. But the spirit voice she contacted was not Sir Conan Doyle. The voice quickly identified itself as the spirit of Flight Lieutenant H. C. Irwin. Flight Lieutenant Irwin had died only two days before the seance aboard the huge British Airship R101 that had crashed in a fiery explosion in the French countryside near Beauvais. Forty-eight out of the fifty-four passengers had been killed in the crash. News of the airship disaster had been in newspapers worldwide, but at the time of the seance the exact reasons for the crash were not known.

As Irwin's spirit described the final moments aboard the doomed airship, Ian D. Coster took down the terrified, nearly hysterical words in shorthand. The voice said:

I must do something about it . . . Engines too heavy . . . Useful lift too small . . . Gross lift computed badly . . . Oil pipe plugged . . . Flying too

low altitude and never could rise . . . Load too
great for long flight . . . Engines wrong—too
heavy—cannot rise . . . Fabric all waterlogged
and ship's nose is down. . . .

During the seance Irwin's spirit gave a long,
detailed account of the many reasons why the
airship crashed. The information was very technical and contained many aeronautical terms
that were completely unknown to Mrs. Garrett
or anyone else present at the seance. After the
seance, Ian D. Coster published the amazing
story of Mrs. Garrett's contact with Flight
Lieutenant Irwin.

Walter Charlton, who had helped build the
airship, was astounded by Coster's report in the
newspaper. Charlton and several colleagues
studied the complete, word-by-word record of
the seance. They found that it contained over
forty highly technical and confidential details of
the causes of the airship's crash. Charlton later
said he thought the idea of anyone at the seance
knowing such detailed information at the crash
was not only impossible but "grotesquely absurd."

Before the official inquiry into the crash, Major Oliver Villiers of the Ministry of Civil Avi-
ation took part in another seance with Mrs.
Garrett. At this seance, the medium was able to
contact other passengers who had died in the
crash. Major Villiers was able to speak to a crew

member who gave more detailed information about the structural problems in the airship that caused the crash. This spirit voice even asked Villiers to refer to a diagram of the dirigible and talked about specific mechanical parts.

Three weeks after the seance, an official inquiry into the crash of Airship R101 was begun. The inquiry took six months and the final report, which was over 450 pages long, confirmed much of the information Mrs. Garrett had received during the two seances.

The testimony recorded during these seances was certainly an amazing moment in the history of spiritualism and psychic research. Because the information Mrs. Garrett received was so technical and because it was later confirmed by aeronautical engineers and the official inquiry into the crash, the case is unique. It presents some very convincing evidence of communication with spirits of the deceased.

CHAPTER SEVEN:
GHOST HUNTERS: WHO THEY ARE AND WHAT THEY DO

What would you do if you thought your house was haunted? Call a ghost hunter, of course. It is not very hard to find one, if you know where to look. Many parapsychologists are experienced at investigating reports of hauntings and poltergeists. A few that we have talked about, like Dr. Nandor Fodor or Harry Price, have become very famous in their field for ghost hunting.

But where would you find a ghost hunter? Well, if your ghost was reported in the newspapers perhaps a ghost hunter would find you. However, the best place to find someone who knows about such matters is at a society or association concerned with the study of paranor-

mal events, such as the American Society of Psychical Research, located in New York City.

THE SCIENTIFIC STUDY OF THE PARANORMAL

The American Society for Psychical Research was founded over a hundred years ago, in 1885. But it is by no means the first organization founded for the scientific study of psychic phenomenon. In the mid-nineteenth century, when Spiritualism was extremely popular throughout America, England, and Europe, several prominent scientists wanted to know if the wonders they had heard about were fraudulent or real.

Dr. Alfred Russell Wallace, a famous naturalist who had helped Darwin develop the theory of evolution, was one of the earliest scientists to study psychic and occult phenomenon. He began his experiments in 1865. Most of Russell's study was with a medium named Mrs. Guppy. In 1867, the London Dialectical Society was formed to investigate the claims of Spiritualism. A few years later in 1870, Sir William Crookes, one of the greatest physicists of the nineteenth century, also announced that he was now turning his attention to researching psychic events. With such prominent and well-respected scientists willing to spend their time in this new territory, other scientists became attracted to the field as well. By 1885, Sir William Barrett and Sir Oliver Lodge, also well-known physicists,

had begun to investigate unexplained psychic events.

Some scientists were completely skeptical and some even wanted to study psychics in order to expose them as frauds. When Sir William Crookes, who had invented several important scientific instruments and also discovered the element thallium, announced to the newspapers that he would study Spiritualism, he added that the use of scientific methods would show that the reports of spirit materializations, floating furniture, and other seance antics were either valid or completely worthless. But Crookes's studies of D. D. Home and a medium named Florence Cook seemed to change his opinion completely.

Sir William Barrett was a professor of physics at the Royal College of Science in Dublin when he first began studying psychic events. His first experiments were focused on hypnosis. He later studied many aspects of Spiritualism, including the many strange events reported during se-ances, such as rappings, spirit materialization, levitation, and so on. He also was skeptical at first of the more dramatic events, such as levi-tation, and believed that such things were best explained as a hallucination of those participat-ing in the seance. Later, however, he changed his opinion after discovering that some of his own friends had mediumistic powers. With their help, he performed tests in broad daylight

and was persuaded that events such as levitation and telepathy were possible.

In 1882, Sir William Barrett founded the Society for Psychical Research. Its goals were to examine a wide range of phenomenon, including hypnotism, apparitions, telepathy, and the events that occurred during seances. On a trip to America three years later, Barrett encouraged the founding of the American Society of Psychical Research. The first president of the ASPR was an astronomer named Simon Newcomb.

The study of psychic phenomenon has always attracted the interest of professionals from a wide range of fields, including physics, psychology, astronomy, and philosophy. There is also a close relationship between psychic phenomenon and philosophical questions. Gardener Murphy, a psychologist who served as president of the ASPR during the 1960s, states that, "Instead of viewing man solely in terms of modern physics and chemistry, psychical research investigates the possibility of new energies, new relations in time and space, which seem to underlie extrasensory perception." It is one of the goals of the ASPR "to expand and improve the full understanding of human nature and the broad scope of human abilities."

In addition to the American and British Societies for Psychical Research, there are many groups worldwide concerned with the study of

the paranormal. Hauntings and poltergeist reports are only a small part of the paranormal events studied by parapsychologists. The list includes ESP (extrasensory perception)—which includes telepathy, clairvoyance, and precognition—psychokinesis, out-of-body experiences, dreams, apparitions, psychic healing, reincarnation, and trance channeling.

WHAT A GHOST HUNTER DOES

If you had a ghost in your house and you called the ASPR for help, you might speak to a parapsychologist named Donna McCormick. Presently the director of ASPR, Donna McCormick has worked at the ASPR for fifteen years. During that time, she has taken part in quite a few ghost hunts. Ms. McCormick said that even when she was very young, she was interested in the paranormal—telling fortunes with cards or tea leaves, or relating stories about ghosts. While Ms. McCormick was studying psychology at Brooklyn College, she volunteered to help with some scientific research at ASPR— experiments having to do with out-of-body experiences. Psychic events had always fascinated her. Now that she was an adult, she could take part in the scientific investigation of such matters.

Ms. McCormick says that the society gets a few hundred calls a year about ghosts and poltergeist disturbances. A large number of these

reports, however, turn out to be explained by ordinary causes or are even imagined by the people who reported them. Sometimes, however, Ms. McCormick decides that the report is worth investigating.

HOT ON THE TRAIL OF GHOSTS

After traveling to the site of a ghost report, the first thing that an investigator might do is interview all the family members and others who have seen the ghost or experienced its presence. As mentioned before, sometimes people do not see a ghostly figure but they do hear footsteps, voices, smell a strange odor, feel a cold draft, or have the sensation that someone is watching them.

Ms. McCormick says that it is hard to rely on eyewitness testimony as totally valid. Like other parapsychologists, she will usually ask witnesses to take a test to measure the accuracy of their perception, along with other psychology tests. The purpose of these tests is to find out if the person is prone to hallucinations or wild flights of the imagination. Parapsychologists also try to find out if the witnesses or anyone in the household has psychic ability.

Ghost hunters will usually bring along certain pieces of equipment. There are two big problems investigators have with using ghost-hunting equipment, however. First, the equipment is delicate, complicated, and cumber-

some. It cannot be moved easily and must be set up in one specific spot. Ghost hunters choose the spot they think the ghost is most likely to manifest itself, but the ghost very well might make its presence known in some other part of a house and they will not be able to record it.

The second problem with trying to detect a ghost using this equipment is that ghosts are often invisible and practically always intangible. Nevertheless, ghost hunters use a video camera equipped to take pictures in low light, and a special kind of audio recorder that can tell what direction a sound comes from. Sometimes an infrared sensor is set up at a spot where the investigators think the ghost might pass. An infrared sensor is basically a beam of light. If something passes through the beam—even something invisible—its passage will be recorded. Since many ghost reports include a drop in temperature or a distinct feeling of cold, some type of thermometer is essential to a ghost hunter. A special device called a themostator measures and records the temperature in a certain location. Sometimes this device will be hooked up to the video and audio equipment so that if the temperature suddenly changes—perhaps because the ghost is present—the camera and recorder will also be activated.

Another type of special equipment that is often used is called a strain gauge. Strain gauges measure amounts of resistance or pressure.

Sometimes they are hung in the air in the area where the ghost has been sighted in order to tell if the ghost's presence is causing a change in the air pressure. A strain gauge can also measure the strength it takes to close a door or window.

Investigators might also use chalk to mark the position of objects in a room so that they can tell if anything moves. They will sprinkle flour or powder in the area being observed in order to detect human footprints or handprints. In this way, they can tell if someone accidentally or intentionally sets off the equipment. If the equipment is activated and there are no marks in the powder, the investigators may conclude that a ghost has been present.

Ghost hunters might also examine maps of the area to see if the phenomenon could be due to natural causes, such as an underground stream that may cause a house foundation to vibrate. They will also make detailed drawings of the various rooms of a house, the property, and the surrounding area. They will examine a house thoroughly and, if possible, study the original plans. Many old houses contain secret cupboards, boarded-up fireplaces, or even hidden tunnels that sometimes account for strange, echoing noises in the night or cold blasts of air.

Investigators also look into the history of the house and its previous owners. They may learn that some unhappy event took place in the

house, or that it was once the site of a church or a prison.

Another problem with hunting down ghosts is that the investigators rarely have a long time to spend in a house or other location where a ghost has been reported. Generally, investigators are not that successful in collecting evidence of a ghostly disturbance, even though they might be present in the house during a manifestation. Ms. McCormick points out that the presence of ghost hunters often inhibits or lessens the intensity of the activity.

She also feels that if investigators could monitor an entire house for an unlimited period of time they would be much more successful in collecting objective evidence of ghostly activity. However, in practically all cases, the family they visit will usually only allow them to set up their equipment for a day or so, which certainly makes the likelihood of observing the ghost very slim.

Ghost hunters will sometimes enlist the help of psychics. A psychic will wander through the house and give his or her impressions of the place and the history of the people who have lived there, or even of the ghostly presence that has been acting up. Sometimes there may even be a seance held in order to communicate with the ghost. Investigators will try to see if these psychic impressions fit into the testimony of witnesses or the house's history.

As you can see, a ghost hunter's job is something like being a special type of detective. Ghost hunters have to be observant and thorough in their investigation.

Ms. McCormick says that ghost hunting can be frustrating. It is very hard to pin down exactly what is going on and why. However, she feels that studying hauntings and poltergeist incidents at the sights where they actually happened is important. But, she adds, this type of investigation has been neglected in recent years by most groups that study the paranormal. One reason may be that it is so difficult to collect evidence from these spontaneous cases. Attention in the field of parapsychology has turned more toward experiments that can be conducted in a laboratory, where phenomenon can be observed under scientifically controlled conditions.

Some people would say that there is already a convincing amount of evidence supporting the belief that ghosts do exist. However, many people remain unconvinced. We may never truly be able to answer the many questions that we have about the topic. Do ghosts exist? Does the human spirit live on after death? Can spirits communicate with living beings? By continuing to search for the answers to these questions, however, we can expand our understanding of the natural world.

INDEX

Foulkes, Maude, 8
Fox sisters
Kate, 63, 65
Leah, 64, 65
Margaret, 63, 65
scientists' investiga-
tions of, 65
Spiritualist Move-
ment and, 63–66
Frost, Judge, 73

Garrett, Eileen
Airship R101 crash
and, 79–82
Green Man investi-
gation, 5–7, 79
Gauld, Alan
J. family investiga-
tion, 41, 44
W. family investiga-
tion, 44, 47
Ghost hunters (para-
psychologists, re-
searchers)
American Society
for Psychical Re-
search (ASPR),
84, 86–88
Barrett, Sir William,
84–86
Crookes, Sir Wil-
liam, 84–86

Fodor, Dr. Nandor,
4–8, 83
Foulkes, Maude, 8
Garrett, Eileen, 5–7,
79–82
James, Professor
William, 71–72,
76
Lodge, Sir Oliver,
72, 74, 84–85
London Dialectical
Society, 84
McCormick,
Donna, 87–88,
91, 92
mediums and Spiri-
tualism, scientists'
investigations of,
65, 69, 71–72, 74–
76, 78–79, 84–86
Murphy, Gardener,
86
Newcomb, Simon,
86
Physical Founda-
tion, 58
Pratt, Professor J.
G., 58
Price, Harry, 25,
79–80, 83
Roll, W. G., 58

Samhain, 10–11
Sauchie poltergeist,
    the, 48–52
Seance(s)
    automatic writing
        and, 69–70
    defined, 30
    descriptions of, 65–
        67, 69–71
    ouija board and, 69–
        70
    at the White House,
        31
    See also Medium(s),
        psychic
Smith, Susy
    Earthbound spirit
        described by, 23
    Eastwind Restaurant
        investigation, 57
    *Haunted Houses for
        the Millions*, 57
    Miami poltergeist
        investigation, 58
Society for Psychical
    Research, 86
Spirits' Book, The
    (Kardec), 60
Spiritualism
    birth and growth of

Spiritualist Move-
    ment, 30, 63–66,
    84
    descriptions of, 30,
        62
    Fox sisters and, 63–
        66
    Rosma, Charles B.
        (spirit), 63–64
    scientists' investiga-
        tions of, 65, 84–
        86
    See also Medium(s),
        psychic; Seance(s)
Stewart, Margaret, 50–
    52
Stone Age legends, 10
Styx, the River, 10

Telepathy, defined, 13
This House is Haunted
    (Playfair), 47
Tower of London, 28–
    30
Tropicana Arts Com-
    pany, 58–59
True Ghost Stories
    (Foulkes), 8
Truman, Harry, 33

The Library of Congress

WHITE HOUSE—Is the White House America's most famous haunted house? According to some, the ghosts of Abraham Lincoln and Dolly Madison have been seen there many times.

The Library of Congress

DOLLY MADISON—wife of the fourth president, while she was living at the White House, planted a rose garden. Mrs. Woodrow Wilson, wife of the 28th president, wanted to have it dug up. Reportedly, the ghost of Dolly Madison appeared and scared the gardeners away. The rose garden still remains.

The Library of Congress

MARY TODD LINCOLN—wife of President Abraham Lincoln, believed that spirits of the dead could be contacted during seances. It is even believed that she held seances in the White House.

The Library of Congress

THOMAS EDISON—inventor of the light bulb and telegraph, was working on an invention that would receive voices of spirits.

The Library of Congress

HARRY HOUDINI—was a famous magician who exposed many fraudalent psychics. Reportedly, Houdini himself had worked as a fake medium for five years before becoming a magician.

London Pictures Service, British Information Services

TOWER OF LONDON—This was the scene of much suffering and unhappiness. Many famous people were imprisoned and executed there. Different ghosts have been seen there.

The Library of Congress

WILLIAM JAMES—the American philosopher and psychologist, was one of the first American scientists to study paranormal phenomena. He observed Mrs. Lenore Piper, a famous psychic medium, and became convinced of her psychic abilities.

The Bettmann Archive

ANNE BOLEYN—the second wife of Henry VIII was beheaded in the Tower of London. She is the Tower's most famous ghost. She has been seen many times with and without her head.